/10

COMPLETE GUIDE TO HUNTING

Nature

COMPLETE GUIDE TO HUNTING

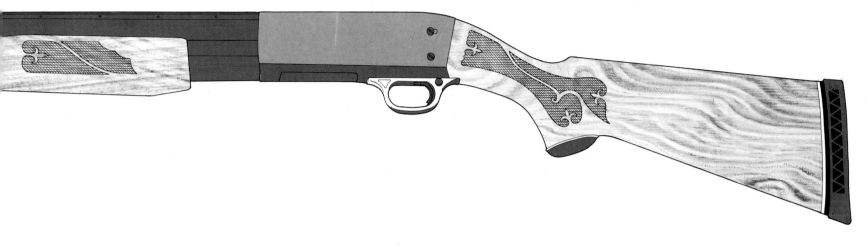

Nature

ROBERT ELMAN / *Supervising Editor*

MASON CREST PUBLISHERS, INC.

COMPLETE GUIDE
TO HUNTING

NATURE

World copyright © 2002
Nordbok International,
P.O. 7095, SE 402 32 Gothenburg, Sweden

This edition is published in 2002 by Mason Crest Publishers Inc.
370 Reed Road, Broomall, PA 19008, USA
(866) MCP-BOOK (toll free).
www.masoncrest.com

Editor-in-Chief: Robert Elman
Cover: Nordbok

 2 3 4 5 6 7 8 9 10
Library of Congress Cataloging-in-Publication Data on file at the Library of Congress

ISBN 1-59084-500-5

Printed & bound in The Hashemite Kingdom of Jordan 2002

Supervising Editor

Robert Elman has participated in the project from its conception, and he has worked closely with the Publisher's editorial and art departments in guiding the authors, editing their material, and collecting the illustrations. Author of over a dozen books on hunting, he has hunted widely, and, as an editor, has specialized in books on hunting and outdoors.

Contents

I Nature

Chapter 1

Man, the Unique Predator

George Reiger

The world of the hunter is the world itself. Everywhere man evolved and migrated, he did so as a hunter.

On the grasslands of Africa and the Americas, only five or six generations ago, men with tools of stone as sharp-edged as a surgeon's scalpel moved with and among vast herds of ungulates, taking from them the bison, wildebeest, and antelope they needed for food, clothing, shelter, and new tools.

On the Arctic ice and in the deserts, where workable stone and wood were in short supply, hunters devised and decorated sophisticated weapons made from the bones and sinews of the seal and walrus, ibex and gazelle that they hunted for food.

In Eurasia, the horse—once hunted for food—was domesticated in the hunt for other animals. In Africa, another hunted species, the camel, was tamed to enable desert foragers to move swiftly from one waterhole, where game was scarce, to another, where more might be found.

In North America, red men hunted camels until there were no more; in South America, red men domesticated the llama and alpaca, but in the process they became herders, not hunters. Elsewhere, men learned to keep pigs, sheep, and goats—although goats particularly would make major and often adverse impacts on local environments when concentrated in numbers beyond the carrying capacity of the land, even as settling down would have significant and often adverse consequences on man's living conditions, sense of community, etc. Man even taught one of his oldest hunting allies, the dog, to be a "shepherd."

Historians have made much of the apparent fact that the wheel was invented in Asia, implying that this part of the world must, therefore, be regarded as the cradle of what we call *civilization*. Since wheelmakers were tillers of the soil, many historians have also concluded that settled agricultural societies were a prerequisite of urban civilization, while nomadic hunters were somehow inferior—incapable of intellectual and creative progress toward civilization.

Yet hunters in other lands were not less thoughtful or creative than wheelmaking Asiatics. They merely had no use for wheels on the tundra, in the mountains, among foothills drained by rivers, in dense forests, or on rock-studded plains and coasts. Some actually carved and attached wheels to their children's toys, but as hunters, they found the sled and the travois, the canoe and the river raft better adapted to their needs and local conditions than wheeled carts would have been.

It is significant that the wheel was invented in conjunction with agriculture, which implies permanent or at least semi-permanent settlement. Of what earthly use would a wheeled vehicle have been to predominantly hunting or herding peoples—Masai or Zulu, Mandan or Sioux—when they could achieve a civilization comparable or superior to that of settled farmers without sacrificing their freedom to roam?

Sixty years ago, H.G. Wells observed that "a certain freedom and a certain equality passed out of human life when men ceased to wander. Men paid in liberty and they paid in toil, for safety, shelter, and regular meals . . . There was a process of enslavement as civilization grew."

And, as civilization grew, it developed a hierarchy of complex and sometimes imaginary needs which required major alterations to the natural world. Forests were cut, rivers dammed, swamps drained, valleys filled, and mountains leveled, sometimes merely to serve the whims of kings and priests or, in modern times, politicians and engineers.

Where hunting peoples had once lived in harmony with the land, they now lived in competition with those who had settled down. And the environment of the hunter was disrupted by his civilized brethren in ways every bit as discordant as changes wrought by geological upheavals and periodic ice sheets.

Agriculture evolved in the tropics and subtropics and generally moved north. In North America, the process of concentrating people into towns and cities began in Guatemala and Mexico. The populations of these countries were supervised by a hierarchy of leaders whose job it was to maintain control as well as to inspire the people to do work that often seemed unnecessary or was sheer drudgery. Since two or three crops of corn, beans, and squash could be produced every year in these warm latitudes, there was no leisure in the Aztec calendar for the common man. Kings and priests used superstition and terror to keep him at his perennial labor.

In the lower Mississippi Valley, a corn economy enabled complex societies to evolve, but winter provided a respite during which hunters could once again follow their immemorial ways, supplementing the society's larder as well as providing skins and sinews for clothing, bones for tools, and fat and tallow for lighting. The religious beliefs of these Mississippi Indians were elaborate and linked with farming, but when times were hard—or exceptionally good—they could be invoked in the making of wars, in which hunting skills were used to take food and treasure from other tribes.

Farther north, as deciduous forests gave way to those of pine and spruce, it became increasingly difficult, and then impossible, to grow crops. Thus, religious ceremonies did not concern the renewal of life in the spring and the harvest of corn in the fall, but celebrated the hunt in all seasons. Priests (shamans) were more like physicians, and belief derived from a community of feeling with animals and wildlife, not from the authority of kings.

It is significant that, in agricultural societies that have evolved a concept of an afterlife, the orthodox view is that life after death is many times better than life itself. However, for some hunting peoples, "heaven" has never meant anything more or less than a continuation of the good, full life on earth.

For the Ojibwa and the Cree, the Creator, who has given a special meaning to each plant and animal, each rock and stream, and who has made existence so beautiful, has prepared an eternal "hunting ground" for all those who respected the red gods.

Natural man—man as he has evolved and as he remains—is a predatory species, despite the gloss of civilization. A recreational hunter learns this, either consciously or instinctively, and as such, man may be thought to

The early North American Indians gave the moose its name and learned to imitate its mating calls in order to lure it within range of their weapons. Later, when Europeans settled the country, they learned from the Indians how to lure the animal which, perhaps more than any other, embodies the remoteness and the majesty of the seemingly endless northern woods.

be most in harmony with, and most comfortable in, his natural environment.

But man is also unique among predators. He is the only predator capable of exercising consciously benign foresight in his interactions with his prey. Various ecological and biological controls maintain the proper balance between other predators and their prey, but no such restraints limit him: his only restraints are self-imposed. Intelligence, self-interest, and appreciation of wild beauty (an emotion that may also be unique to our species) motivate the hunter to preserve the habitat and its other denizens for future generations.

In still other ways, man is different from other predators. Physically, he is inferior not only to them but to his prey. He cannot run or swim or climb as fast; he cannot pursue winged prey through the air; he has far less stamina than most prey, less strength than some; his hearing is relatively poor; his eyesight is ill adapted for dim light; his scenting ability is almost nil; and his capacity to withstand cold, heat, hunger, and thirst is unimpressive. Yet he is the most efficient of all predators.

His brain and technology are such that he can, if he chooses, devastate all prey. But he also has a conscience—probably linked closely with his aesthetic appreciation—and thus he can evolve as a benign predator. Likewise, his brain and technology enable him to survive visits to the wilds and thoroughly enjoy the experience, while his foresight and conscience urge him to preserve them as a crucial habitat for all creatures, including himself. Yet it is his civilization—urbanized, industrialized—that diminishes the game and threatens to engulf the remaining habitat, which is the habitat of man himself.

Hunting for pleasure, the oldest sport on earth, is also the most natural: a direct and atavistic interaction with nature. When in tune with its surroundings, it does not destroy them. Man has long hunted in this way and always will, if other activities do not annihilate flora and fauna alike. But today, hunting is limited and must be stringently regulated, because for many centuries man has abused the animals and their habitat.

The decline of game is not precipitated by regulated hunting. It results from the destruction of the natural environment and the wanton extermination of wildlife. Industry is rapidly pre-empting vast expanses of

11

swamp, savanna, delta, prairie, tundra, taiga, and even the most productive habitat of all, the rain forests. The African veldt and the North and South American plains are being plowed and fenced. Asian and Mediterranean wetlands are being dredged for commercial navigation or filled and paved for factories. All of these ecosystems are crucial for the survival of wildlife.

Today, industry—the word was once associated with personal skill and diligence—touches every land and all bodies of water on earth, even those unsuitable for agriculture. It is able to modify environments that the farmer cannot use. Tracts of land in the far North, in the deserts, on remote islands, or in the mountains—where hunting peoples had until recently seemed to be beyond the grasp of industry—are now exploited by corporations whose executives may never visit any of these places. The resources they want are not those that the local people need.

Especially hard-hit is the Eskimo. The culture of this quintessential hunter was safe so long as there was nothing known to be commercially useful in the Arctic wastes. Now the industrial world's thirst for oil has sent the shadow of civilization across even the stark, white lands of the North. Traditional skills and perceptions seem meagre beside the world of the computer, kayaks are traded for outboard-powered skiffs, and sled dogs are replaced by snowmobiles. Chickens grown thousands of miles to the south now feed men who once hunted walrus and seal from fragile boats made from the hides of the hunted.

Still, there are a few who cling to a way of life and an understanding of nature more ancient than the oldest wheel. "There is only one great thing," sings an Eskimo hunter, "to live, to see the great day dawning and the light that fills the world."

Yet there are also people from the industrialized world who are working diligently to protect fragments of these distinct and diminishing habitats on the plains, prairies, and deserts; in the rain forests and mountains; and along the rivers and coasts. They are carrying on the work begun more than a century ago in Europe and North America by sportsmen/naturalists, who began to attempt to preserve portions of their vanishing wilderness.

Natural diversity is not just a fashionable phrase. It is essential to man's continued well-being and possibly to his existence as a species. Hunters learn the value of diversity, and the rules of conservation which guard diversity, at such an early age that they often assume that the world already knows what the hunter perceives.

But the civilized world has largely forgotten the lessons of the hunt.

While extinction has always been part of the pattern of evolution, in recent industrialized centuries, the pace of wildlife extinction has accelerated alarmingly. In the nineteenth century, 75 bird and 27 mammal species vanished. So far in the twentieth century, 53 bird and 68 mammal species are gone, and there are 345 bird, 200 mammal, 80 amphibian and reptile, and an incredible 20,000 to 25,000 plant species currently threatened with extinction.

Some hunting peoples have had a little, but not much, to do with this. We know, for instance, that after the Polynesians came to New Zealand about the tenth century, their descendants, the Maori, had killed the last indigenous swan (*Cygnus sumnerensis*) by the fifteenth century, and had also killed the last moa some two or three hundred years later.

American Indians always killed animals for food but may have contributed to the extinction of the mammoth and the mastodon by driving them over cliffs, killing many more animals than could be utilized. They may also have contributed to the extinction of several other species that were failing to adapt to new environmental conditions following the withdrawal of the Laurentide glacier after the last periodic Ice Age. They hunted bison, too, but killed only for need. It was not until the beginning of the 1870s that the railroad opened up the plains of North America to market hunters. They shot the bison and sold the meat (often

In the rain forests, the abundant natural growth of trees, bushes, other plants, and seemingly parasitical vegetation allows virtually no space for deliberate cultivation. The peoples that make the forests their home do so only by sharing them with a huge range of fauna—birds, beasts, reptiles, insects, and fish—and by finding or hunting whatever they need for their survival. Shown below is a man of the Vedda tribe, Sri Lanka.

(Above) Man is all but confined to the lowest levels of the rain forests. Above his head rises layer upon layer of life, which exist at different levels. Beneath his feet is perhaps the thinnest and most amazing layer of all: the shallow tropical soil, which can be so quickly washed away once the protecting forest that it supports is cut down. (Top right) The world distribution of rain forests. (Right) A tropical rain forest in northern Queensland, Australia.

Of the main types of vegetation in the world, illustrated below, the tundra *(1)* produces least growth per unit of area per year (see diagram, right). The tropical rain forests *(8)* produce more than eighteen times as much. Between these two extremes lie the coniferous forests *(2)*, the deciduous forests *(3)*, the steppes *(4)*, the subtropical forests *(5)*, the deserts *(6)*, and the savannas *(7)*.

When the annual growth of each zone is compared with its standing crop, a different picture emerges. On the arctic tundra, the annual growth accounts for no less than twenty percent of the total standing crop. In the tropical rain forests, the figure is just under seven percent; in the coniferous forests of the middle taiga, just over three percent; and in the proverbially slow-growing oak forests, just over two percent. On the temperate steppes, by contrast, the annual growth is as much as forty-five percent of the standing crop, and in the subtropical deserts only a little less, at forty-two percent.

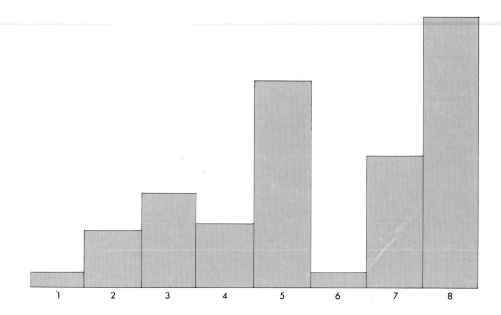

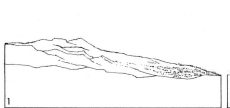

only the choicest parts) to frontier settlements, railroad camps, and army garrisons. Bison skins were sold for tanning and the bones for fertilizer. Furthermore, huge hunts were organized for the recreational hunters that helped further to destroy the great herds.

Yet, during the nineteenth century, *recreational* hunters had begun the revolutionary task of preserving wild and scenic areas as a means of preserving threatened fish and wildlife species. Their start in North America would have been more difficult, were it not for the fact that, as a class, sportsmen were, and are, largely members of the industrial elite that earns profits from the development and exploitation, ironically enough, of many of the very wildernesses they seek to set aside. In the ranks of these early preservationists were many cultural and political leaders, which meant that the word *conservation* became respectable far sooner than it would have if the revolution in environmental appreciation had been led by intellectuals alone.

In the British Isles and continental Europe, recreational hunters were mostly of the landowning class, who hunted, shot, and fished on great estates—privately-held tracts of woods, fields, waters, and mountains. Those who owned the land and the game on it were, very largely, of the aristocracy that had once been feudal. For the landed gentry, conservation was not a new concept but merely an aspect of land ownership with a tradition already centuries old. It was obviously a facet of managing one's property adequately to pay competent gamekeepers and to manage the habitat and the game as renewable and profitable resources.

Habitat improvement, selective shooting, supplemental breeding and feeding of game when necessary, predator control (including ferocious

laws against poaching), closed seasons, and other techniques of conservation all contributed to the tradition of private ownership that has ensured that game is still available in Europe, despite its ever-growing, ever more urbanized populations.

In Africa and Asia, recreational hunters, regardless of whether they were of the landed gentry or not, were members of the exploiting class; some were empire-builders, but all saw what seemed an infinite wilderness—limitless game in unbelievably productive habitats. They saw no need for management of the game or the land, and so African and Asian wildlife diminished at an astonishing and steadily accelerating rate.

The crumbling of European empires did not reverse the trend, for the remaining game was regarded by the peoples of the emerging nations as sorely needed food or detrimental to agriculture—or both.

Only very recently have strenuous efforts been made by a few African and Asian governments to conserve the wildlife of the savannas, the plains, and the rain forests of these continents. Here, too, as in North America, enlightened self-interest has at last spawned a conservation ethic, for wildlife is a tourist attraction, and tourism has been touted as a salvation for the economies of some African and Asian nations.

In North America, most of the land was obtained by treaty from the Indians and, as in Africa, its resources seemed limitless. In the decades after the Civil War, a few far-sighted visionaries who fortunately wielded enormous influence sparked off a concern for conservation in their writings and legislative proposals.

For some creatures, the effort was not in time. The cutting of the vast forests in the eastern half of the United States was probably the most

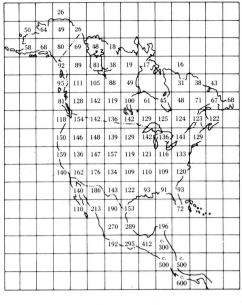

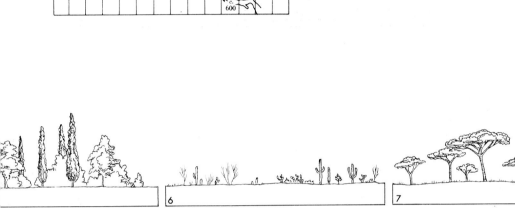

(Left) The grid imposed over the map of North and Central America shows the numbers of breeding land-bird species in different parts of the continent. This shows a range from only 16 in the north of the Northwestern Territories of Canada, to over 400 in southern Mexico; in Ecuador, on the northwest coast of the South American continent, there are seven times the number of bird species as are found in New England, or over 800.

The same pattern may be observed for other creatures and plants in other parts: Europe has 192 species of fish, while over 1,000 have been recorded in the Amazon basin. A deciduous forest of 4 acres in Michigan will contain 10 to 15 species of trees, while the same area of tropical rain forest in Malaya may contain up to 227 different species. (Krebs, *Ecology*. New York, 1972.)

significant factor in the demise of both the passenger pigeon and the Carolina parakeet. Neither species was an important target for sportsmen. The passenger pigeon was mostly shot in large numbers by commercial gunners and pioneers, and the parakeet was usually the victim of angry fruit growers whose crops were ravaged by this beautiful bird when it switched its diet from acorns to apples.

The essential habitat of both species had been the great deciduous canopy stretching from the Atlantic to the Mississippi and from upland Georgia to New England. Once that was cut into patch-quilt remnants of its former ubiquity, there was no way the passenger pigeon and the Carolina parakeet could survive.

A similar process involving many more species is seen today in tropical rain forests. The recreational hunter has long been intrigued by what he loosely calls "the jungle," and former American president Theodore Roosevelt was, in 1914, not the first sportsman to explore the rivers of Brazil and to hunt for jaguar, tapir, and other game.

Partly because of Roosevelt's concern, Barro Colorado Island, created by flooding associated with the construction of the Panama Canal, was made a sanctuary and a scientific research preserve. The island is nearly 3,000 acres (1,200 hectares) in area, with a sizable tract of rain forest. Yet the island is apparently not large enough, for its list of unique flora and fauna has been shrinking steadily for over half a century.

Every minute of every hour of every day in the year, about 50 acres (20.5 hectares) of tropical rain forest are being destroyed. The original area of rain forest on earth was roughly 6.2 million square miles (15.9 million square kilometers). By 1975, this area had been reduced to 3.6

million square miles (9.3 million square kilometers), and at the present attrition of 92,500 square miles (245,000 square kilometers) per year, our grandchildren will never be able to visit a tropical rain forest.

Although such conservation groups as the World Wildlife Fund, supported in part with sportsmen's money, are making every effort to set aside representative tracts of rain forest before it is all gone, the vital question is: how much is enough?

Rain forests contain more species than any other ecosystem on earth. Between twenty-five and fifty percent of all plant and animal species on earth are found in this environment. Yet no tropical rain forest is older than about 10,000 years.

How did this incredible diversity of life develop so rapidly? Do creatures in the rain forest have a low extinction rate, or are rain forests just amazingly conducive to the emergence of new species? Perhaps both are true, for certainly rain forests permit more species to live in harmony with one another than any other environment (except the somewhat comparable oceanic "kelp forests").

Even though we have barely begun to study such phenomena, we are losing rain forests faster than even our best instruments can collect data about them. The red soil of the tropics is curiously infertile, and the farmer who clears a tract in the jungle must abandon the land within a few years unless the soil is reinforced annually with chemical fertilizers (a cost beyond the reach of most subsistence farmers). Furthermore, such red soil does not easily reproduce the lost rain forest. We do not know how rain forests came into being, and we are unable to reproduce them (except at fantastic cost) once they are gone.

The grasslands of Africa cover a large part of the continent from below the Sahara to South Africa. The type of grassland varies from semi-desert and torrid steppe (on the periphery of the Kalahari and Sahara deserts) to the savanna of the equatorial regions to the veld of South Africa. The annual rainfall and the periods during which the rain falls are major factors in deciding what type of grassland an area will have. The savanna supports a wide variety of herbivorous animals that live together in relative harmony, as each species has its own food patterns and/or eats at levels that the other species cannot reach. Highest up comes the giraffe, and then comes the

elephant. The gerenuk *(1)* stretches up on its hind legs to reach the intermediary levels. The gazelle *(2)* and the topi *(3)* crop at the grass at its lowest level; the zebra *(4)*, the gnu *(5)*, the white rhino *(6)*, and the Cape buffalo *(7)* are all grazers; some crop close, others crop at the tops of the various grasses. The black rhino *(8)* prefers twigs and bark, while the dik-dik *(9)* eats the lowest leaves on bushes. These herbivorous animals support predators, such as lions (a lioness is shown here with a newly killed gazelle), and scavengers, such as vultures and hyenas, shown here eating carrion. The hyena is also a predator.

(Right) This savanna has recently received an abundant fall of rain. Trees and grasses are flourishing, and the area is capable of supporting a wide variety of animals. The flat-topped acacia trees are a familiar sight on savanna grasslands.

A major question involving this destruction of the world's rain forests is the effect on the earth's climate and geography as the estimated 340 billion metric tons of carbon stored in the wood fiber of rain forests are released through cutting and burning. Even cautious scientists speculate that, in addition to warming world temperatures so that the polar ice caps will shrink and the oceans rise by many meters, the grain-producing potential of western North America will vanish due to generally drier summers. In addition, the forests absorb carbon dioxide and give off oxygen to an extent that might make our survival somewhat dependent upon theirs. Therefore, we can say without any hesitation that the preservation of natural environments is considerably more important than merely being a nice way for wealthy sportsmen to make tax-deductible, charitable donations.

Major and permanent alterations in the world's climate are too much like science fiction for most people to take them seriously. However, wildlife and habitat preservation can be put in another, more immediate context. For example, when people learn that the armadillo is currently being studied as part of man's search for a cure for leprosy, that the albatross may provide a cure for heart disease, the black bear for kidney failure, and the manatee for hemophilia, wildlife conservation makes the most urgent kind of sense.

Furthermore, a wild flowering plant called the foxglove, found in Europe and Morocco, is the sole source of the drug digitalis. Without it, between 10 and 20 million people would die within seventy-two hours of heart failure. People are less inclined to shrug at the idea of endangered plants. And when you ask why fewer than 20 plant species produce ninety percent of the world's food, when nearly 80,000 plant species are edible and nutritious for man, you may start a few wheels turning in the minds of people who had, perhaps, taken a high-protein diet too much for granted.

During the past century alone, many species have become extinct, and although people nowadays are more aware of the importance of conservation, there are many other, once-plentiful species that are now rare or even in danger of extinction. Illustrated here is the now-extinct passenger pigeon, which once existed in millions in North America.

18

Chapter 2

The Hunter's Role in Habitat Preservation

George Reiger

The musk-ox is an animal of the arctic regions. Originating in Asia, it wandered over the land bridge that once connected Alaska and Siberia. Protected since 1917 in Canada and 1950 in Greenland, it now appears to have a secure future, although recent Norwegian attempts to implant the animal in Spitsbergen have failed.

In 1978, in the over-populated state of Jalisco, Mexico, a unique species of corn was discovered to have the same number of chromosomes as our domestic variety. Its uniqueness lies in the fact that it is a perennial plant; it does not wither and die with the coming of winter, but from year to year produces tiny ears of corn on stalks. When this species is crossbred with our larger hybrid species, corn on the cob can be harvested from plants tended much like blueberries and pineapples, which are grown without the increasing annual expense of spring planting.

This fabulous discovery was made in an area where the plant was assumed to be just another weed. In fact, this area of scrubland, host to dozens of bird species and several non-migratory mammals, was slated for clearing and development. Had that happened without a proper analysis of the area's resources, all mankind would have lost infinitely more than could have been satisfied by building a few more housing units for Mexico's ever-burgeoning human population.

Even after we have domesticated or synthetized a product of nature, we are foolish to turn our backs on its origins. This happened during the 1960s after pharmaceutical firms had become over-confident that the malarial preventive they were marketing in substitution for natural quinine, which is derived from the bark of South America's cinchona tree, was sufficient for any malarial threat. However, when warfare escalated in Southeast Asia, the *falciparum* malarias of that region took an increasing toll—until natural quinine was reintroduced as a more potent antidote than its imitation.

The world is running out of petroleum, and the price per barrel keeps rising. This has set off a frantic search for natural and artificial substitutes. Several plants, among them the widespread euphorbia tree of equatorial latitudes, may provide some relief. An acre of euphorbia trees, under which other plants grow and wild game grazes, will yield ten to fifty barrels of oil per year at a cost that may be economic or even profitable.

How is all this related to hunting? Simply and directly. Just as primitive peoples in South America had known about the curative powers of quinine long before they were discovered by civilized Europeans, equally primitive people of Africa and Australia taught modern scientists about oil in the euphorbia, a characteristic which makes this tree superb for starting campfires but almost too rich and smoky for cooking.

These examples are further related to hunting because sportsmen were among the first to perceive that an arboretum doth not a forest make, and wild creatures in a zoo are no longer wild.

Since, in hunting, the act of killing is momentary compared with coming close to the animal in its own environment, the recreational hunter has always been concerned more with the perpetuation of species as a whole than with the artificial propagation of remnant individuals in zoos. The hunter knows that *habitat preservation is central, not just to the perpetuation of wildlife, but to the preservation of his own well-being.*

An example of wildlife preservation is the North American pronghorn antelope. Pre-Columbus, the pronghorn and the bison together dominated the ecosystems of the western prairies and plains. Each numbered perhaps 30 or 40 million. Their food and water requirements differed subtly enough for them to complement each other. Yet by the turn of the twentieth century, the pronghorn is estimated to have numbered only some 13,000 animals. By 1927, it was being hunted in only three states.

Wildlife management since then, however, has ensured a stable population today of some 400,000, with hunting seasons for *Antilocapra americana* in sixteen western American states, two Canadian provinces, and one Mexican state. Nearly 2 million head of pronghorn have been shot since 1927 without jeopardizing the species.

Today, cattle have replaced the bison on the grasslands, and there is little likelihood that bison will be restored beyond the relatively few token herds that exist, since the environmental needs of cattle and bison are identical. However, pronghorn occupy a niche in no way competitive with cattle, and as ranchers have gradually come to appreciate this fact, the pronghorn has flourished.

The comeback of the American elk, or wapiti (to distinguish this member of the deer family from the European elk, or moose), has been more limited than the pronghorn's, because the wapiti's habitat requirements make it impossible for the species to adapt to life with man in so many regions preferred by both them and us. Although small herds exist in Michigan, Pennsylvania, and Virginia—all part of the wapiti's historic range—the subspecies that used to roam through these states, *Cervus canadensis canadensis*, is now extinct.

However, in the West, wherever room still exists, the wapiti thrives. It is presently hunted in nine American states and three Canadian provinces. Colorado alone estimates that wapiti hunters contribute more than $40 million to the state economy. License fees account for one-tenth of this total and go directly into wildlife management and research programs.

Although the dollar value of the wapiti harvest is a fraction of that of the whitetail-deer, cottontail-rabbit, or mourning-dove harvest in the United States, just seventy-five years ago, there were probably fewer than 25,000 wapiti in existence. That population figure now represents less than one-fourth of the annual harvest.

Unfortunately, we may be at the apogee of wapiti restoration. This animal is essentially a creature of the wilderness. With the current boom in backpacking and camping, non-hunters are inadvertently forcing wapiti out of many favored summer ranges. In addition, increasing numbers of hunters indicate an interest in shooting at least one "elk" in their lifetime. However, this commitment is casual, and hunting pressure continues to build only in the most easily accessible parts of the wapiti's range—a factor detrimental to the quality of local herds—while, on the other hand, there is insufficient hunting for wapiti in more remote areas, a factor equally detrimental to the quality of remote herds. North American advances in game management are admired by wildlife authorities throughout the world; yet here is a case in which the Americans might do well to emulate the selective-shooting system of game management that has long been in force in Europe.

Increased logging poses yet another threat to big game, and habitat acquisition is becoming increasingly expensive. Finally, wildlife management itself is belittled by many people who are opposed to hunting, and research is discouraged or extremely difficult in officially designated American Wilderness Areas.

At one time, the wapiti was approaching extinction because the animal was slain for a pair of incisiform canine teeth in the forward part of the upper jaw. These "whistlers," "buglers," or "elk teeth" were especially prized by members of the Benevolent and Protective Order of Elk (BPOE), an American social fraternity, which paid such high prices for

(Right) Wide, seemingly empty stretches of undisturbed countryside, far from urban and industrial concentrations: such is the typical national park. Shown is a national park in northern Sweden. Human activity here has been largely organic and has consisted of reindeer herding and subsistence fishing by the Lapps.

(Below) No matter how remote or undisturbed a wilderness is, it is accessible to modern methods of transportation, for instance the helicopter *(1)*. With energy at a premium nowadays, an undisturbed waterfall *(2)*, even in a national park, can be exploited for electricity, permanent means of access *(3)* being built. Soon, another part of the wilderness will have vanished beneath the waters of a hydroelectric dam *(4)*.

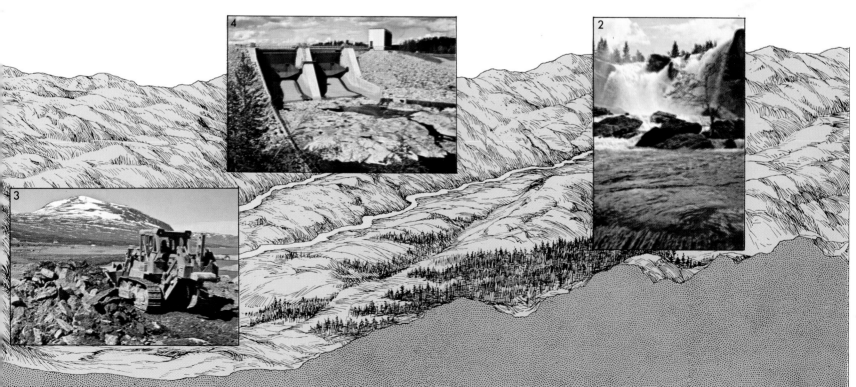

Breeding only once in about every four years, the Indian rhinoceros *(1)* is perhaps typical of the four other surviving species: the black rhinoceros *(2)*, the white rhinoceros *(3)*, the Java rhinoceros *(4)*, and the Sumatra rhinoceros *(5)*. While these unurgent reproductive habits suggest a long evolution into a peaceful, unthreatened existence, they can hardly explain the attribution of sexual potency to rhinoceros horn. It is a grotesque irony that this belief should combine with human population growth to threaten all species of rhino with extinction.

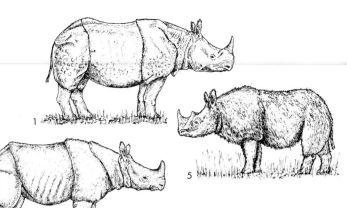

(Right) The anatomy of an Indian rhinoceros: *(1)* the "horn" is, in fact, a growth of hair-like material, supported on a structure extending forward above the upper jaw. The upper lip *(2)* projects in a finger-like extension similar to that on the extremity of an elephant's trunk.

these biological anomalies that wapiti were slain by the hundred for their teeth alone.

Equally bizarre is the current slaughter of rhinoceros for their horns. While the rhino was always considered to be a trophy animal because of its size and the danger inherent in collecting a specimen, trophy hunting *per se* was never a threat to the survival of the various rhino subspecies. Habitat destruction and horn hunting have become such a threat today.

Rhino horn is now literally worth its weight in gold. Whereas a decade ago there were 20,000 black rhino in Kenya, there are presently fewer than 2,000.

The horn is normally powdered and used in potions alleged to cure everything from leprosy to impotency. In north Yemen, it is carved into dagger handles, for which wealthy Arab sheiks pay $10,000 (£5,000) each. Poachers run enormous risks by sneaking into national parks, tracking the animals at night, spearing them, sawing off the horn, and escaping before dawn—risks far too great to be worth taking for the relatively little money they are paid for the contraband by middlemen, who buy and sell the horn several times before it reaches the consumer as an alleged aphrodisiac or as a decorative item.

Still, a Kenyan park ranger earns only $56 (£28) a month, while a poacher is paid over $100 (£50) per lb (0.5 kg) for a horn that averages nearly 8 lb (almost 4 kg). The risks notwithstanding, it is a wonder that more rangers do not become part-time poachers! Perhaps the fact that some illegal buyers in Nairobi pay nearly $400 *per ounce* for rhino horn shames the rangers into trying to purge this scandal from their land.

Their efforts to date, while often more risk-filled than those of the poachers, have not been enough, although recent reports indicate that black rhino numbers are at last beginning to grow. Although Kenya is a signatory to the international treaty banning trade in endangered species and their products, fourteen of the eighteen African nations where the rhino survives have *not* signed the treaty; and China, a principal market for rhino-horn powder, has only recently agreed to sign.

In the Ngorongoro Crater in Tanzania, there were 76 black rhinos in 1978; 26 in 1979; and possibly none today. In all of Africa, there are only an estimated 10,000 to 20,000 black rhinos; approximately 3,000 southern white rhinos; and less than 500 northern white rhinos.

In Asia, barely 1,135 Indian rhinos survive, and increased poaching and habitat conflicts between man and rhino threaten even this small number. Sumatra may have 225 rhinos left, and Java maybe about 50. Since a female rhinoceros produces only one calf every four years, there is no way normal procreation can keep pace with the poaching.

One of the ironies of the East African problem is that it has become so much worse since regulated recreational hunting was outlawed some years ago. Not only were rhinos worth many times more to local economies when hunted as trophies than their horns alone are worth today, but the presence of recreational hunters on safari helped to prevent much of the poaching that is currently possible, because there is no way for the meager East African game-protection staffs to patrol all the areas where rhinos are in jeopardy. In bygone days, every "white hunter"—that is, professional hunter/guide—was also a deputy warden, and poachers were more afraid of them and their camp staffs than they are of the vague and arbitrary justice of Kenyan or Ugandan law today.

Despite the fact that it is unlikely that this generation of sportsmen will have the opportunity to hunt rhino, sportsmen continue to give generously of their time and money to preserve this marvelous species which, after the elephant, is the largest of all land animals. Wildlife enthusiasts who are not hunters themselves are eager to contribute to saving "Flipper" the dolphin and "Blubber" the whale, but there is no such popular

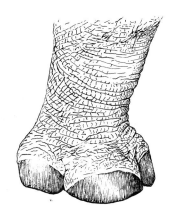

(Below) The rhinoceros is a three-toed animal. Much of the bearing surface of the foot comprises the thick horn that protects an elastic pad in the foot, which cushions the impact of the animal's weight.

upsurge of feeling for the rhinoceros. It is a magnificent brute, but its magnificence can best be perceived by those who have hunted it.

Thus, it is not surprising to learn that the World Wildlife Fund is funding the effort to save the rhino from extinction. Since its founding in 1961, the Fund has allocated over $40 million (£20 million) to 1,800 wildlife research and habitat preservation projects in 131 countries. It has helped to create or support 260 national parks on five continents and has helped to save 33 endangered species of mammals and birds from extinction. Let us hope its drive on behalf of the rhino comes in time.

Most people still see the preservation of wildlife as a matter of maintaining threatened or endangered species in small parks and zoos. They confuse the salvation of a few token individuals with the general perpetuation of species. By contrast, and intrinsic to the hunter's recreation, is the understanding that a healthy population of any species is a result of natural selection, in which the weakest die of disease, parasites, or the attack of predators, leaving the strong to further the species; evolution never stands still. Natural diversity implies that there be enough food, water, and other requirements for a given species in its preferred ecosystem; but it also implies that there will be competition as well.

This is why the hunters long ago began to form habitat preservation and restoration societies. Although the American National Audubon Society is not normally regarded as either a hunter-affiliated organization or a land-preservation group, its early membership and direction were provided in large part by hunters who established the pattern for habitat preservation that makes this organization the largest non-profit and non-governmental land steward in North America.

In more recent decades, the Nature Conservancy—again, with many hunters in its leadership and ranks—has provided additional momentum to habitat protection and, most recently, has begun to focus on the dilemma of the rain forests in Central America and the Caribbean.

Although Ducks Unlimited (DU) owns no land, it has leased hundreds of thousands of acres in Canada for the protection of wetlands and the perpetuation of wildlife dependent on wetlands—including dozens of birds and mammals that will never be hunted by the waterfowling contributors of DU.

Likewise, in the British Isles, the Waterfowlers Association of Great Britain and Ireland (WAGBI) supervises not just the instruction of young hunters and the protection of game species; it is in the vanguard of efforts to save imperiled wetlands in these two nations.

Throughout the world, recreational hunters are playing a leading role in the protection of the natural environment so essential to the well-being of man as well as wildlife. Sportsmen are ridiculed or harassed by ignorant people; their importance to conservation's past, present, and future is often maligned by anti-hunters determined to rewrite history, so that the recreational hunter will have played no role at all.

But to exclude the hunter from history is to deny mankind its roots—roots which still supply us with all the vital ingredients of life and evolution. Man is a predator by ancient design. Unlike the ducks or deer he now hunts, he possesses eyes set for optimum three-dimensional vision—like those of the peregrine falcon and the great cats, our fellow predators. Our jaws and teeth were developed not for living on roots and berries alone. We were obliged by nature to be hunters, and so long as there is game to hunt, there will be hunters.

ROE DEER (*Capreolus capreolus*)

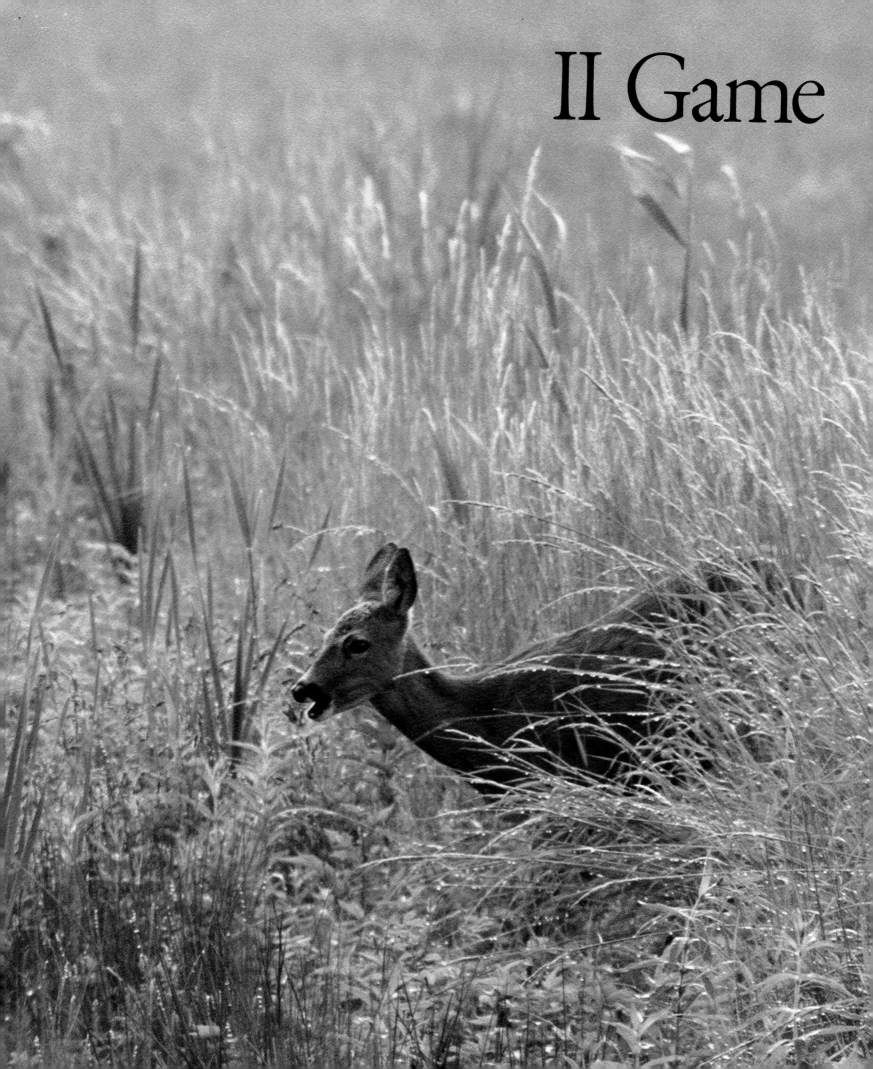

II Game

Chapter 1

European and North American Game Animals

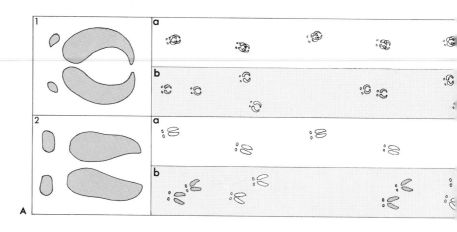

Caribou, or Reindeer *(Rangifer tarandus)*

This is an animal of the sub-polar regions, and while there are a number of subspecies, the principal division is between animals that live above and below the tree line; the former, perhaps not surprisingly, are generally smaller. Caribou is the only species of deer of which both bulls and cows have horns of more or less the same size, those of the cows being slightly lighter than those of the bulls. Another feature, but not one so readily noticeable, is the animal's pelt, which is light, thick, an excellent insulator, and waterproof; the animals can survive winter temperatures of –40°C (–40°F) but have trouble dissipating heat in summer. Neither prolonged rain, nor even swimming, causes their skin to become soaked, while the air-retaining qualities of the pelt make it very buoyant.

Reindeer—the word derives from Old Norse—are most associated, in Europe, with the Lapps, who maintain semi-domesticated herds that range unhindered, except for human intrusions, over most of northern Scandinavia and into Russia. The animals are found all the way east through Siberia. In North America, the animal is called caribou—a word that came into English from French, and derives from an American Indian language—and has been important to some Indian peoples, and vital to the Eskimo of North America and Greenland, for food, clothing, shelter, tools, and weapons.

The woodland subspecies do not migrate or range extensively, at any rate not nearly to the same extent as the barren-ground or tundra subspecies. These move in spring and fall between winter and summer territories that may be 600 miles (1,000 km) or more apart; they do so in herds that can be enormous: as many as tens or even scores of thousands of animals. They tend to make use of the same migration routes and the same calving grounds year after year and are thus particularly, if not very apparently, sensitive to human intrusions into their territory. Any sort of permanent construction—the Alaska pipeline is the best-known recent example, but by no means the only one—may disrupt the breeding and migratory habits of the animals.

Apart from men, the reindeer's natural predators are wolves, bear, wolverine, and lynx, which prey mostly upon stragglers from the herds; weak, sick, and injured animals are thus eliminated. Calves are often taken, but they are most at danger from cold, wet weather in spring.

The mating season is in late summer and early fall, and calves are born, after a gestation time of about eight months, in late winter or early spring. Calves are usually single, but twins occur; they can follow their mothers after only some twenty-four hours.

The largest caribou in North America are the Osborne caribou (*R. t. osborni*), of the Rocky Mountains and have massive antlers. They are generally classified as a woodland species, and others, elsewhere in the world, are the woodland reindeer of Scandinavia (*R. t. fennicus*) and the

Siberian reindeer (*R. t. sibericus*). Woodland caribou are found across the whole of northern Canada, but their real stronghold is in the east, and the best trophy heads are from the interior of Newfoundland.

Barren-ground reindeer (*R. t. tarandus*) in North America and Greenland include a number of geographical subspecies. The main one is the Greenland (*R. t. groenlandicus*), found from southern Greenland to the MacKenzie River a little to the east of the Alaska border. West of the river, and westward into the Yukon and Alaska, is the home of Grant's caribou (*R. t. granti*), the largest of the barren-ground animals. To the north, across the Arctic islands, and into northern Greenland is the range of the small, pale Peary caribou (*R. t. pearyi*), and it is estimated that there are about 25,000 of them; as well as their coloration and size, their antlers are distinctive, being almost upright.

A few wild reindeer (*R. t. tarandus*) still exist in the mountains of Norway and Karelia in Finland, but most are now owned by Lapps who mark them for ownership with a complicated arrangement of cuts in the ears. [GG]

Moose, or European Elk *(Alces alces)*

These animals—the largest members of the deer family *Cervidae*—are huge, quite unmistakable beasts with immense, spreading, palmated horns, a drooping nose, and almost grotesquely long legs. In their element—the marshy forests of the north—these great deer move like shadows, specters of a seemingly vanished past. Their American name, moose, derives from the Narragansett name for them—moos.

They have a circumpolar range, like the reindeer, but further south. The European species (*A. a. alces*) is now found chiefly in Scandinavia, where it is known as elk; it can weigh up to about 1,200 lb (540 kg). Further east is the Siberian species (*A. a. pfizenmayeri*) of northern Russia, and it is comparable in size to the Alaskan moose. A smaller subspecies, the Manchurian moose (*A. a. cameloides*), is found in eastern Asia.

The North American species is led, in size, by the Alaskan moose (*A. a. gigas*), which is almost black, can stand 7½ feet (230 cm) at the shoulder and weighs up to 1,800 lb (800 kg); its horns are proportionally large and are therefore the most sought-after trophy. It ranges through the wooded regions of Alaska, the western Yukon, and northwest British Columbia. A much smaller, pale variety occurs in the Rockies, the Shiras moose (*A. a. shirasi*), which only seldom exceeds 1,000 lb (450 kg) in weight.

Elsewhere in North America, moose are either of the eastern or northwestern subspecies, respectively *A. a. americanus* and *A. a. andersoni*. Bulls weigh about 1,000 lb (450 kg), but the average is lower; the northwestern is slightly larger, and ranges through Canada from western Ontario to the Pacific and north to the Beaufort Sea above Alaska, and

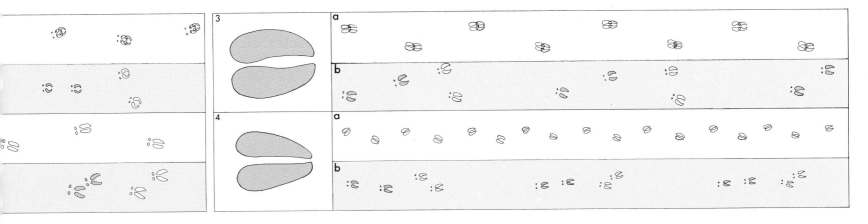

across the northern parts of Wisconsin, Michigan, Minnesota, and North Dakota. It overlaps with the eastern moose, which inhabits the forests of eastern Canada, and, in very small numbers, those of remote areas of the northeastern United States.

All moose need woodlands with bogs and marshes and, while they prefer deciduous trees for food, they will also eat coniferous shoots and buds. If these are scarce, as often may be the case in spring, moose will graze on early spring crops. In warm weather, they eat aquatic grasses and other such vegetation and can sometimes be seen flank-deep in lakes or even submerged, like a hippo. They can swim well, too.

They mate in September and October, the cows calling to the bulls with a loud, bawling noise. The bulls fight, sometimes with fatal results, but do not maintain harems. They shed their antlers during the winter, growing new ones during the spring and summer. Gestation takes some eight or nine months, and calves are thus born mostly in May; twins are common, and calves remain with their mothers for a year. While the cows are hornless, their size makes them formidable, and they resent intruders when they are with very young calves. Bulls in rut become blindly furious and commonly work off their rage on trees: they have been known to charge locomotives. While hunters might shoot them at this time, perhaps in self-defence, the flesh of a bull in rut is not good to eat. At other times, by contrast, it is prized, being tender and succulent, and, of course, there is a great deal of it. In the far north of North America, and in much of Scandinavia, the meat is a significant part of a winter's food supply; the annual legal cull in Sweden, for example, is nearly 100,000 elk of an estimated population of over 300,000. Many are killed on the roads there, too, and their very bulk and dark coloration make them a deadly menace for motorists at night. While the Scandinavian population of elk has been growing steadily for some years, as towns absorb more and more people, in North America the southern parts of the moose's range have shrunk from the intrusion of human activity. [GG; TT]

Red Deer (*Cervus elaphus*)

The red deer stag is the pre-eminent hunting trophy of Europe and, as such, has been celebrated for centuries in art, literature, and music. Called *Hirsch* in German, the animal was formerly reserved for noblemen only on the continent of Europe, while, in Britain, its strictly legal status was vague until after World War II. The North American red deer (*C. e. canadensis*) is known as the wapiti, or elk.

Red deer now occur westward across Europe from the British Isles to Russia, wherever there are the deep forests that the animals like. The exception is the treeless forests of Scotland that still hold many red deer; these areas were still heavily wooded in the first half of the eighteenth century, and have retained their deer and names, but not their trees.

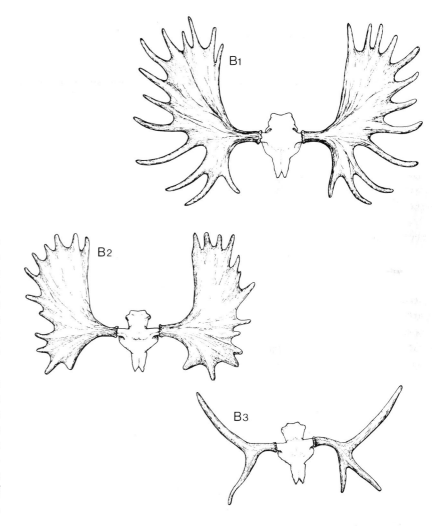

A Deer tracks in soft earth or thin snow can be distinguished from one another. *(1)* Caribou have markedly rounded hoof-prints: *(a)* walking, *(b)* running. *(2)* Moose have asymmetrical hooves that are roughly parallel when the animal is walking *(a)* but spread out when it is running *(b)*. *(3)* Red deer tracks. *(a)* When the animal is walking, the hind feet overprint the marks of the front feet. *(b)* When running, the dewclaws, or lateral hooves, leave clearly visible marks. *(4)* Roe deer tracks are similar to, but smaller than, those of red deer. *(a)* Walking. *(b)* Running.

B The horns of moose and European elk are of different sizes and forms. *(1)* Moose's are generally larger; this is an example of the palmated type, with "fingers" spreading out from a "palm." *(2)* European elk, palmated form. *(3)* European elk, cervina form. All sorts of variations between palmated and cervina types occur.

(Above) **FALLOW DEER** (*Dama dama*).
(Center) **MOOSE** (*Alces alces*).
(Below) **CARIBOU, or REIN-DEER** (*Rangifer tarandus*).

(Right) **WAPITI** (*Cervus elaphus canadensis*).

An average red deer stag of central Europe weighs about 275 to 300 lb (125 to 135 kg), stands about 4 feet (120 cm) at the shoulder, and measures about 6 feet (180 cm) in total length. A pair of antlers—a head—may have up to twelve points; it is then called a royal. Exceptionally, an eighteen-pointer head has been known. Red deer are larger in Eastern Europe than anywhere else, while those of Scotland, which live on exceptionally poor land, considered agriculturally, are smaller. Hungary, Czechoslovakia, and Yugoslavia all have good populations of large deer. Those of West Germany are smaller in average size, but their numbers are impressive, having been maintained by that country's superb game-management endeavors.

Red deer can adapt to new habitat and have done well in numerous transplantations. New Zealand, for example, now has a large population in isolated areas, and there are healthy herds in parts of South America and Asia. A few red deer have been imported into North America, perhaps inadvisedly, for they have competed with domestic species—whitetail and mule deer, and wapiti—for browse and cover in habitat continually being reduced by human activities.

Red deer are gregarious and form large groups, normally led by an old hind and consisting of hinds, calves, and young stags; the older stags usually congregate in smaller bachelor herds throughout much of the year. The rut—the breeding season—begins towards the end of September, being heralded by the roaring of the stags as they identify and challenge one another; the sound resembles that of a roaring lion. The stags fight by butting one another; curiously, stags with antlers having only a single point, or altogether without antlers, are most likely to overcome their rivals. Well-developed heads of horns seem superfluous in these rutting struggles and, if they become entangled and locked together, the stags can starve to death. [TT]

Roe Deer (Capreolus capreolus)

Roe deer, compared with red deer, are diminutive: a mature buck weighs about 50 to 65 lb (23 to 30 kg) and stands about 28 inches (70 cm) at the shoulder. Bucks have antlers that have at most six points; does rarely have horns, which are always small. Bucks and does have a rich foxy-red coat in summer; in winter, it turns grayish and can be flecked with yellow. There can be many color variations while, in the Netherlands and northwestern Germany, melanistic—i.e., black—roe deer can occur. In winter, a white rump patch develops, and the species has special muscles that can cause the patch to expand into a disk, to form an alarm signal. The tail is very small, hardly visible. In winter, the does develop a tuft of long hair, called the anal tush, which is sometimes mistaken for a tail; it can be a useful way of distinguishing does from bucks that have shed their antlers.

There are two types of roe deer, the field roe and the forest roe, and the latter is far more common. It prefers small woods, ideally those that are bordered by meadows or fields, for this habitat provides ample shelter and an optimum food supply. The field roe prefers open fields and can obtain the shelter it needs from even the most meager thickets and brush. Even in heavily populated countries, the deer population can be considerable. In West Germany, for example, some 60,000 deer a year are killed accidentally on the roads.

Distribution elsewhere in Europe is southward from Norway, Sweden, and southern Finland to Spain, Portugal, and Greece; the species stretches eastward to Iran and the Ural Mountains. In the British Isles, the species was at one time nearly extinct but is now abundant, having been extensively introduced out of its original areas. East of the Urals and throughout much of Asia, the European roe is replaced by a somewhat larger subspecies, the Siberian roe (*C. c. pygargus*), while another subspecies, the Chinese roe (*C. c. bedfordi*), is found in China and most of the Korean peninsula. [TT]

(Above) The development of the roe deer's horns. *(1)* Winter months. *(2)* February. *(3)* March-April. *(4)* June-September. *(a)* First point. *(b)* Second. *(c)* Third.
(Below) The red deer's antlers. *(1)* First or second year. *(2)* Second year. *(3)* Third year. *(4)* Fourth year. *(5)* Fourth or fifth year. The ten-pointer. *(a)* Brow antler. *(b)* Bay. *(c)* Tray. *(d)*
Fork. *(6)* The twelve-pointer, or royal. *(a)* Pedicle. *(b)* Brow. *(c)* Bay. *(d)* Tray. *(e)* Tine. *(f)* Palm. *(g)* Top. *(7)* The fourteen-pointer. The crown *(a)* may develop several more points. *(8)* The sixteen-pointer. After this, the antlers will almost certainly go back, although eighteen-pointers have been recorded.

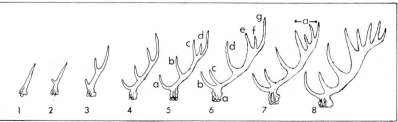

Fallow Deer *(Dama dama)*

Originally a native of Mesopotamia, in the valleys of the Tigris and the Euphrates, the fallow deer has been successfully introduced into many other parts of Europe. It now occurs in the wild in virtually all European countries apart from some—Belgium, Holland, Italy, Norway, Portugal, and Switzerland—where it is preserved in parks and private estates. Transplanted herds thrive in the wilds of New Zealand, on private hunting preserves in North America, and in the wild in eastern Kentucky and in other parts of the southeastern United States, where wildlife agencies have studied the possibility of establishing fallow deer in huntable numbers.

Smaller than the red deer, a mature fallow stag weighs about 200 lb (90 kg) and stands about 3 feet (90 cm) at the shoulder. Unlike almost all other deer, fallow deer have spots on their pelts when mature, a feature that is particularly noticeable when their pelts take on their characteristic reddish-brown summer coloration. Fallow deer exhibit a much wider range of color variation than do most species of deer: from almost black to a light yellowish-brown. Wholly white and wholly black specimens have been observed. The common name of the species—fallow—indicates what must have once been its predominant color, a pale brownish or reddish yellow.

Only the bucks have antlers and—another unusual feature of the species—they are palmated, like those of the European elk. Perhaps semi-palmated would be a more accurate description, for the horns grow from the head in the normal, unpalmated fashion, but on mature bucks, definite palms do develop at the top of the antlers.

Typically for European deer and some other animals, fallow deer are larger in size (and antler dimensions) the further east they live; the best heads and the largest deer are to be seen in Czechoslovakia, Rumania, and Russia. There is a subspecies known as the Persian or Mesopotamian fallow deer, which occurs in southern Iran; as this is the area from which fallow deer were first transplanted, by the Romans, these deer may be the only examples of the original form still existing in the wild.

Fallow deer are less sensitive to the presence and activities of people than are red deer, for fallow deer are usually satisfied with small woodlots and sparsely forested areas, even in areas of high human population density. While they are often found living together with populations of red deer and roe deer, they seem for some reason—perhaps competition for mast and other foods—to avoid areas with a high boar population. Fallow deer have been suggested as "the deer of the future" for Western Europe, but it is unlikely to become as popular with hunters as the red deer. [TT]

Whitetail Deer *(Odocoileus virginianus)*

These deer range in size from bucks of 200 lb (90 kg) and more in the upper Northeast and Midwest of the United States, to the tiny Florida Keys whitetail (*O. v. clavium*), which would be exceptionally large at 80 lb (36 kg). An even smaller variety is reported from Coiba Island, off Panama. Apart from these two small subspecies, whitetails are much alike, despite having been divided by taxonomists into some thirty subspecies, of which seventeen are found in the United States.

The deer now occur in North America east of the Rocky Mountains. Their northern limits are determined by winter cold and snow conditions. While their gray-brown pelts give good protection against cold, snow deeper than about 3 feet (1 m) is really too much for them, but they have, in fact, reached the James Bay area at the south of Hudson Bay and the Peace River Valley of Alberta, a bare 400 miles (640 km) south of the Arctic Circle.

They flourish on the abandoned farms of the northeastern United States, where their population has been reckoned to be as high as fourteen deer to the square mile. More southerly states, such as Alabama

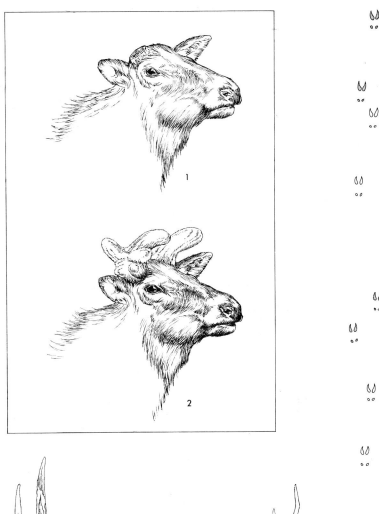

The antler development in the wapiti, the North American red deer. *(1)* In March, the pedicles are just visible. *(2)* After three months, the budding horns are covered with velvet. *(3)* In August when the antlers are fully grown, the velvet covering becomes itchy, and the bull rubs it off on trees and bushes.

The tracks made by a wapiti in flight are also shown. They are similar to those of the whitetail deer.

and Texas, have high populations, and various subspecies range through Mexico and into Central America.

Whitetails do well in immature wooded areas, for these provide the food and cover they need; historically, they have spread with the cutting of the mature forests of the eastern United States, for these lacked brushy undergrowth and branches low enough for the deer to graze on. They eat practically anything vegetable and, on cultivated land, will dig up root crops such as beets and carrots and will enter orchards to eat the apples off the trees. With this adaptability, it is hardly surprising that their population in North America is as high as 10 million.

During the warm summer months, the deer grow fat, the fawns gather strength, and the antlers of the bucks develop. By late October, when the rut begins, their antlers have been scrubbed clean of velvet on bushes. Bucks do fight among themselves, but only briefly and without harming each other; their antlers can, however, lock together and then both bucks will starve to death.

The species is polygamous, and bucks attract does by establishing a series of "scrapes." They scratch the earth clean of leaves and vegetation, then scent it with urine and musk from the tarsal glands. Each buck may have several secluded scrapes and, at the peak of the rut, he will visit them regularly.

Shortly after the rut, whitetails start a gradual migration to their wintering areas. This can entail a move of anything from a mile to a hundred miles or more (2 to 160 km); distances tend to be short in the south and long in the north.

In the south, wintering areas are loosely defined or not defined at all, whereas in the north, where snow can drift to depths exceeding three feet (1 m), the deer depend on "yards" for survival and trample out deep runways to and from food and shelter through drifts that would hopelessly bog down a single animal. A "yard" is an easily recognized wintering area, usually on a south-facing slope, in a valley, or in some other sheltered spot. A yard that is overcrowded can provide insufficient food if the weather turns severe; even if many deer die, the remainder seem unwilling to move on as a group or to disperse.

By March, the strains of winter begin to show, for the deer that survive become gaunt and ragged by early spring; this is especially marked with the yearling fawns, which are too short to reach such food as is available, and, during the most severe winters, all the yearling fawns may not survive.

By April, the snow banks melt, and the survivors can begin to roam and gorge themselves. The fawns are born, spotted and almost scentless. [GG]

Mule Deer (Odocoileus hemionus)

From Mexico to Alaska, Rocky Mountains mule deer (O. h. hemionus) or one of its ten subspecies are found just about everywhere in the western half of North America. Each of them is adapted to its own particular niche—from the arid Mexican plains to the windswept ridges of southeastern Alaska—and, with the exception of the two races known as blacktail deer (see below), all have about the same life pattern.

A distinguishing characteristic of all mule deer is their large ears and, on a big buck, they can be as long as 12 inches (30 cm), measured from their base. Some experts maintain that the ears serve to dissipate excess body heat. The animals are typically barrel-bodied with stocky legs; they have short white tails tipped with black. Their antlers are formed of a number of branches, rather than a single branch with spikes growing off it. Of all mule deer, the Rocky Mountains "muley," as they are affectionately called, has the largest spread of antlers and is the most prized trophy. An adult buck will weigh about 400 lb (180 kg).

These deer are migratory, spending summers at altitudes sometimes exceeding 8,000 feet (2,400 m). From about the middle of September, the

(Opposite, upper) **MULE DEER** (*Odocoileus hemionus*).
(Opposite, lower) **WHITETAIL DEER** (*Odocoileus virginianus*).

(Below) Whitetail deer running, and showing how well their name describes them.

deer descend along well-worn trails of their own making to winter pastures; the deer in the southern part of the range do not migrate, however.

Breeding takes place toward the end of October and, while the deer congregate in groups of bucks and does, they do not form harems, as some other species do, nor do the bucks fight as much. Fawns are born after a gestation period of about seven months; does produce single fawns in their early breeding seasons but, later, commonly produce twins or even triplets. The fawns are born when the deer have returned to their summer pastures; the bucks move there first, followed shortly afterward by the does heavy with young.

Mule deer may live as long as twenty years, although the average life span is about ten years. They were formerly much preyed on by cougars and wolves, but these predators are now scarce. Coyotes, bears, and lynx may take an occasional deer, but the adult mule deer are large and formidable antagonists. [GG]

Blacktail Deer (*Odocoileus hemionus columbianus*)
(*O. h. sitkensis*)

These two subspecies of mule deer inhabit the Pacific coastal forests of

(Below) The mule deer. Movements of the black tip against the contrasting white of the rump make a vivid signal that is visible at a great distance. The species got its common name from the animals' huge ears.

(Below, inset) The blacktail buck stretching up to browse can be identified by the large extent of black on its tail.

North America, ranging from southern California to Vancouver Island—the Columbian Blacktail—and thence northward through the vast off-shore archipelago of Queen Charlotte Islands and into the Alaskan Panhandle—the Sitka blacktail. They differ in a number of respects from the mule deer.

Their tails appear black—they have a white underside—and are flared, while those of the typical mule deer are cylindrical. The Columbian is slightly darker and slightly smaller than the average mule deer, while the Sitka is darker and smaller still. A pale brownish-yellow variety occurs in the deserts of the Southwest, but, otherwise, blacktails are deer of the forests and mountainous brush country.

Like whitetails, they are elusive and crafty and, when they do not flee, running flat-out, they can "freeze" into immobility, even when a hunter or his dog is in the neighborhood, or move noiselessly away. While mule deer typically run with a bounding motion, blacktails bound only occasionally.

They swim well and have thus spread out over the British Columbian and Alaskan archipelago, which is now over-populated with them. Once, cougar, wolves, and lynx kept down their numbers, so that the deer did not exhaust their own food supplies, but this is now what curtails populations, especially in severe winters, when many blacktails can starve to death.

They thrive best in areas of new growth, such as may be found after forest fires or lumbering operations. Although they have been observed to be faithful to a given territory, despite pressures of hunting, the biggest concentrations of deer occur in these new growth areas.

Their breeding season begins in mid-September in the south of their range and in November in the north. Fawns are born after a gestation time of about seven months and twins are so common that this is really the rule. [GG]

Pronghorn (*Antilocapra americana*)

A mature buck weighs up to 145 lb (65 kg) and will then stand 41 inches (105 cm) at the shoulder. Both sexes are horned, and the bucks' horns may grow to a length of 20 inches (50 cm), but 12 inches (30 cm) is the average. One peculiar feature of the bifurcated horns is that they consist of an inner core and an outer sheath, the latter shed annually. The horns of the females rarely exceed a length of 3 inches (8 cm).

Pronghorns are russet to dark brown and have white underparts. The face and front of the neck are patterned in black, brown, and white. If it is scared, the animal erects the long, white hair on its rump patch.

Pronghorns belong to the western parts of North America, where they occur from southern Alberta to northern Mexico. During the winter, they live in large herds, which break up into smaller ones in spring. A herd of the smaller type usually consists of an old buck with up to eight hinds and their young. The younger mature bucks then congregate in bachelor herds. The rut takes place in September-October, and the gestation period lasts eight months. The hinds commonly give birth to one or two young. Pronghorns generally live in open, dry grassland and avoid forests. They mainly eat grass, herbs, moss, and lichen. [RE]

Mountain Goat (*Oreamnos americanus*)

This animal is an antelope and is distantly related to the antelopes of Asia and Africa but does its best to live up to its name: it looks and acts like a goat, and lives in the mountains like one, and so acquired its name from the first Europeans who saw it.

It is found only in North America, occurring in the high mountain peaks of southern Alaska, the Yukon, and the Northwest Territories south through British Columbia and Alberta into Washington, Montana, and Idaho. There are small herds in Wyoming and the Black Hills of South Dakota.

It has a strikingly thick, white coat with long guard hairs. The males, or billies, weigh from 200 to 300 lb (90 to 135 kg), and the females, or nannies, are slightly less heavy. Both are horned, and while the horns of some nannies are longer, those of the billies are thicker and more massive.

Mountain goats can keep their footing on almost imperceptible small ledges, outcroppings, and bumps as they cross practically vertical cliffs. They appear to be able to walk up vertical rock walls and successfully to defy gravity. Their hooves are unique in that they have a spongy portion that grips almost like a suction cup, but, despite this, occasional mishaps do occur. Indeed, falls from heights, and rockslides, account for a far greater number of fatalities than all other causes combined—predators, disease, hunting, and shortages of winter food.

Nannies and kids stay together in herds of up to a dozen animals, while the billies are solitary, or gather in small bachelor groups, except in November, which is the start of the mating season, and in winter. They feed principally on grass from high mountain meadows.

Billies become pugnacious in the mating season. Kids are born from April to June and, while single births are most common, twins do occur.

During winter, the goats seek lower elevations on southerly exposed hills, where the wind has swept away the snow; in spring, they move back into the peaks. [JK]

Bighorn Sheep *(Ovis canadensis)*

Bighorn sheep have spectacular, heavy, curving horns and inhabit high mountain country that is as magnificent as the sheep and that would seem barren without them. The bighorn is North America's most coveted trophy.

Bighorns are divided, for purposes of scoring trophies and establishing records, into two classes: Rocky Mountains bighorn and desert bighorn. There are, a little confusingly, different geographical variations, too, for example, the Californian bighorn.

The animal's range extends from central British Columbia and Alberta south through the western mountains into northern Mexico and Baja California. The arid hills of Nevada, California, New Mexico, Arizona, and northern Mexico, including the Baja, comprise the habitats of the desert bighorn, which is less numerous and slightly smaller than the mountain bighorn.

Both rams and ewes have horns, but the ewes' are smaller, lighter, and lack the complete "curl" of the rams'. Mature mountain rams may weigh up to 300 lb (135 kg), but 250 lb (113 kg) is a more usual weight; the ewes are about three-quarters the size of the rams.

Bighorns are generally brown with pale snouts, rump patches, and bellies. Mountain bighorns tend to be dark brown, while the desert variation may be as dark, but is mostly a lighter tawny or buff color that blends well with its surroundings.

The breeding season is in late October and November. The rams mate with as many ewes as possible. The older, stronger rams keep the younger ones away from the ewes. Spectacular butting jousts are common between antagonistic old rams. These battles are almost a ritual. Accidents do occur in which one of the opponents is hurt, but this is rare. After the breeding season, the rams lose their jealousy and antagonism for one another and form bachelor herds apart from the ewes.

Winter is a hard time for sheep. As the first snows come, the sheep move down from the high mountain meadows of 9,000 to 10,000 feet (2,700 to 3,000 m) to pasture at 2,000 to 3,000 feet (600 to 900 m). The better winter ranges always have southern exposures and are regularly swept free of snow by the wind. In the spring, the sheep return high into the mountains.

One of the problems that affect bighorn sheep is that their winter pastures are frequently grazed over by domestic sheep and cattle in the

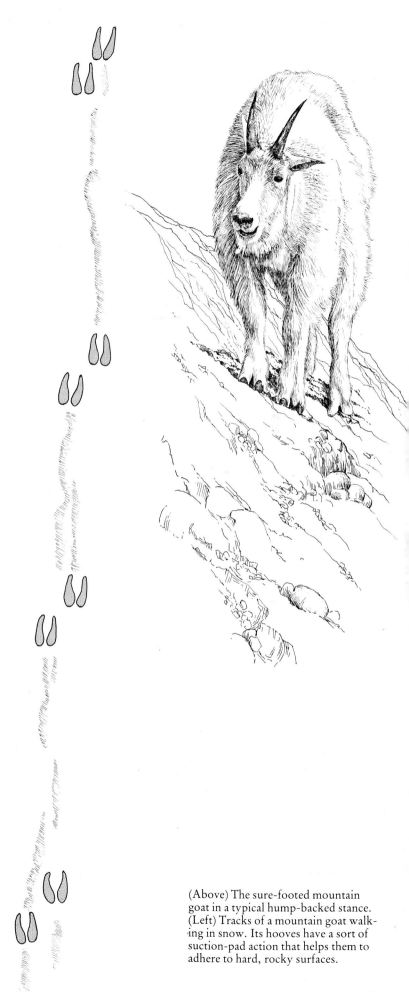

(Above) The sure-footed mountain goat in a typical hump-backed stance. (Left) Tracks of a mountain goat walking in snow. Its hooves have a sort of suction-pad action that helps them to adhere to hard, rocky surfaces.

(Left) **BIGHORN SHEEP** (*Ovis ca-nadensis*).
(Left below) **MOUNTAIN GOAT** (*Oreamnos americanus*).
(Far right) **DALL SHEEP** (*Ovis dalli*).
(Below) **MOUFLON** (*Ovis mu-simon*).

summer months. When the bighorns descend into lower elevations in the winter, they must contend with overgrazed pastures. [JK]

Dall Sheep *(Ovis dalli)*

The Dall sheep is a wild sheep of Alaska, the Yukon, and the Northwest Territories, while its subspecies, the Stone sheep (*O. d. stonei*), is found in the mountains of northern British Columbia.

The coat of the Dall is white, and its horns are thinner in structure than those of the bighorn, and they flare out at their tips. Like the Stone, the Dall is sometimes referred to as a "thinhorn."

The Stone sheep is dark gray to almost black, and its horns are somewhat heavier than those of the Dall, while having the same shape and structure. Stone sheep horns are separately classified in the trophy records, and it is worth noting that the biggest wild-sheep horns, the famous Chadwick head, are of a Stone sheep.

Both Dall and Stone sheep have essentially the same life history as the bighorn, although Dalls do not seem to make so great a seasonal migration as do bighorn sheep. After the rut, the rams and ewes stay more or less together for the entire winter, and, when spring comes, the rams separate into bachelor groups.

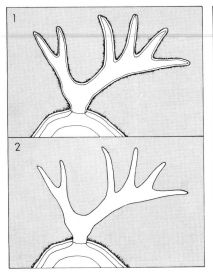

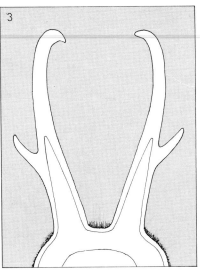

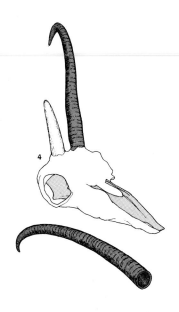

Some horned animals—red deer, for example—grow and shed their horns annually. *(1)* During the period of growth, the horns, which grow out from the skull, are covered with skin. *(2)* Later, this falls away or is rubbed off against trees and saplings. *(3)* Bovids—cows and antelopes are of this class—have hollow horns that grow around a core of bone. These horns are not shed, and grow longer year by year. Shown are an exception, the horns of the pronghorn, which sheds its horns, but not their cores, annually. *(4)* The skull of a chamois, showing the core of bone protruding from the skull.

Dall sheep have less trouble in winter than bighorns, for they live in more remote areas and seldom have to compete with domestic livestock for winter grazing. Their population is greater, too, and the number of hunting licences issued annually is greater. [JK]

Mouflon *(Ovis musimon)*

A relatively rare animal on the continent of Europe, the mouflon was introduced there from Sardinia and Corsica. It has adapted successfully to the hilly hardwood forests of Central Europe, particularly in areas of dry rocky terrain. It has also been successfully established on the Hawaiian island of Lanai. Like red deer, mouflon require a fairly large area within which they can satisfy their instinct to roam.

Mouflon are in many ways similar to the bighorn sheep of North America, but they are considerably smaller, an average German specimen weighing only about 100 lb (45 kg). They stand about 30 inches (76 cm) high at the shoulder. In winter, they are dark brown, with parts of their bodies being almost black.

They feed primarily on herbs and grasses, and cause practically no damage to trees or crops. They roam as they feed, returning to particularly favored meadows in the late afternoon.

Ewes and lambs herd together, being led by an old ewe. Rams, on the other hand, are solitary. Mature rams may, however, band together for a time, but not during the rut. This occurs in November and December; then, the rams rejoin the herd and battle with one another for possession of harems. Those that are unsuccessful roam restlessly during this time.

The distinguishing feature of the mouflon is, of course, its horns; this is so for all species of wild sheep. As many mouflon rams do not develop horns with a spiral, only really good trophies closely resemble those of the bighorn sheep. A common, and so less desirable, type is of horns curving in a long graceful sweep outward from the head, then in toward the neck. [TT]

Chamois *(Rupicapra rupicapra)*

Related to, but smaller than, the North American mountain goat, the chamois is an antelope which is found in similarly high terrain, primarily in the Alpine region but also, in smaller concentrations, in other, lesser mountain ranges. It is only sometimes found below the timberline.

It stands about 2½ feet (76 cm) high at the shoulder and is about 3½ feet

(107 cm) long. A mature male weighs about 75 lb (34 kg) and a mature doe some ten percent less. In winter, both are dark brown to black, but, in summer, somewhat lighter brown. The face is yellowish-white, marked with a dark stripe from the ear to the nose, over the eye.

Bucks and does are horned, and both are hunted as trophy animals. They are among Europe's most sought-after game animals. The horns, which are never shed, curve rearward toward the head, the buck's with a pronounced hook. The doe's are somewhat smaller.

The German for the animal is *Gams*, thus giving the name *Gamsbart* to the highly prized trophy consisting of a thick brush of the hair from the spine of a mature chamois. This hair is plucked, not cut, and formed into a fan or mushroom-shaped brush which adorns the hat, forming part of the traditional dress of the inhabitants of the Alpine region. No self-respecting Bavarian seems to feel that his or her wardrobe is complete without one such hat. [TT]

Ibex *(Capra)*

This is a family of European wild goat, of which there are two species, the Alpine ibex (*C. ibex*) and the Spanish or Iberian ibex (*C. pyrenaica*). Some eight varieties exist and differ chiefly in the size and shape of their horns. However, it is only in the Pyrenees and in Spain that sufficient numbers of ibex exist to make hunting practicable; some 30,000 Spanish ibex are said to inhabit the Pyrenees and the central mountainous region of Spain.

Through intensive game-management programs, the Alpine ibex, or *Steinbock*, as it is known in the German-speaking parts of Europe, has been re-introduced into the Alpine regions of Switzerland, Austria, Germany, Italy, and Yugoslavia. Before this was undertaken, the animal had been reduced to near-extinction, with a small colony remaining in the Italian Alps, and another, smaller one in the mountains around Salzburg.

Both species of ibex are short and stocky, and males reach a weight of 230 to 240 lb (105 to 110 kg). Their horns are so large in proportion to their bodies that they seem ungainly. Those of the Alpine ibex are the longer, attain a length of nearly 40 inches (100 cm), are set close together on the animal's head, and curve back in a simple arc; they have a triangular cross-section and heavy knobs or ribs on the front-facing surface. The horns of the Spanish ibex are slightly shorter, tend to a lyre shape with a slight curve towards the tips, and lack the knobs of the Alpine ibex.

Ibex are proverbially agile climbers, and this goes for the newborn kids, too; they can follow their mothers without difficulty only a few hours after birth. In summer, ibex graze on high-altitude mountain vegetation, and they move down the mountains when snowfalls begin, to feed on whatever grasses and lichens there are.

Ibex breed from about October to December, during which time the billies fight furiously among themselves. A gestation period of some five months causes kids—almost invariably single—to be born in spring. [TT]

Wild Boar (Sus scrofa)

Wild boar are still found in Europe eastward from West Germany and, like the red deer, the animals become generally bigger as one goes eastward. The average weight of males in West Germany, for example, is about 200 lb (90 kg), while in Turkey, it is almost 400 lb (180 kg). Wild boar are not only omnivorous, but destructive, too, and the damage that a herd can do to a grain or potato field in only a single night is almost unbelievable. In the more densely populated agricultural areas of Europe, they have, therefore, been hunted relentlessly, but the species is by no means near extinction.

They are also nomadic, so much so that they are omitted from the annual game census required by West German law. They usually keep close to heavy thickets that provide escape routes, if need be, and while they will cross open, dry areas, it will only be when they are moving from one place to another. They forage at night, and the chances of seeing wild boar by chance during the day are slim. They are, therefore, usually driven when hunted.

Wild boar are armed with formidable tusks, protruding for up to 8 inches (20 cm) from either side of the snout. When charging, boar do not detour round anything, not even a hunter. Their tusks are very sharp, and hunters have been known to take refuge in handy trees to avoid them. It has been debated whether or not boar are naturally aggressive, or "only" given to trying to escape as fast as they can on such occasions but, in the field, it is probably advisable to jump first and debate later.

Wild boar were transplanted to North America first in the 1890s, again in 1910 and 1912, and yet again in 1925. Naturally, some of the animals escaped and spread out into the surrounding countryside, often interbreeding with stray domestic pigs or their feral relatives, so the coloration of wild boar in North America is now more variable than that of their European cousins. Weights vary from about 200 to about 350 lb (90 to 160 kg), with the heavier animals being generally of the least intermixed wild strains. [TT]

Brown, or Grizzly, Bear (Ursus arctos)

In Europe, the brown bear exists in small numbers in the Pyrenees, the Alps, the Balkans, and northern Scandinavia; it is also found in Russia and Asia. In North America, despite the diminishing areas of wilderness available, there are healthy numbers of grizzly and Alaskan brown bears. Scientists now classify all of these bears as the same species, but of different geographical races. This is not entirely satisfactory from the North American point of view, as no one knows where the grizzly's range ends and the Alaskan brown's range begins, and the best way to distinguish between these two may be to speak of the grizzly as the inland bear and of the Alaskan brown as the coastal bear.

The range of the inland (grizzly) bear extends from the mountains of Wyoming, Montana, and Idaho north through British Columbia and western Alberta, and through the western part of the Northwest Territories, the Yukon, and the interior of Alaska. The Alaskan Brown (coastal) bear ranges from southern Alaska—including, of course, Kodiak Island, which is famous for the size of its bears—southward into British Columbia. The coastal bear is bigger than the grizzly because it eats more protein and fat. It is famous for catching and eating salmon, both live fish on their way up the coastal rivers to spawn, and dead fish that fail to survive spawning. The female coastal bear—female bears are known as sows—weighs between 500 and 800 lb (230 and 360 kg); fully grown males—boars—range from 800 to 1,200 lb (360 to 540 kg) and can exceed that, too. One of the largest on record weighed over 1,600 lb (752 kg) and was nearly 9 feet (274 cm) long. Incidentally, it is the skulls of bears, not the skins, that are used to rank them in the famous Boone and Crocket Club trophy records, as skull dimensions are a reasonably reliable indicator of a bear's size, whereas skins can be stretched.

The inland bear does not have access to such large quantities of rich food as the coastal, and it is consequently smaller: sows weigh from 400 to 600 lb (180 to 270 kg) and boars from 500 to 800 lb (230 to 360 kg).

The pelt of U. arctos varies in color from dark brown to almost blond or russet. Inland bears frequently have white-tipped guard hairs, hence the name "grizzly."

Brown bears are omnivorous. Apart from fish, they eat all kinds of vegetation, wild fruits, berries, grass which they graze like cows, and all sorts of small animals—rodents, birds, reptiles—which they catch or dig out of their holes. They eat insects, too, and have been observed swimming, mouth open, in streams where water-borne larvae were plentiful. Bees, grubs, and the proverbial honey need scarcely be mentioned. Bears will kill and eat larger animals, and eat carrion: moose, deer, caribou, elk, wild sheep. Old boars have been known to eat even bear cubs.

Salmon of five different species spawn in the rivers of the Pacific Northwest and, as they spawn at different times, it is possible for bears to eat salmon most of the summer. Even inland bears eat fish when spawning runs occur in inland rivers and streams; their other food is most abundant in late summer and early fall, and it is then that they are most likely to be seen by the hunter, for they are active then and spend much time above the timberline, foraging for food in order to accumulate fat for their winter dormancy.

The first big snow of late fall or early winter drives them to their dens. They do not hibernate in the strict sense of the word, as their body temperature does not fall. In the early spring, the bears emerge from their winter dormancy. The adult boars are the first to emerge. Sows with cubs, which are born during the dormancy or which are from the previous year's dormancy, come out last.

On emerging in spring, bears still have rich and glossy pelts, with no patches of hair rubbed out. At first, they feed on grass, so the place to hunt them is on grassy hillsides and mountain meadows. Most bears shot in the spring are shot by hunters who have packed into the mountains with pack horses or have scouted from boats along coastal inlets and rivers.

The brown bear is an animal of the wilderness. Its continued existence depends, therefore, on there being enough wilderness available for it; undeniably, its range is on the decrease. [JK]

Black Bear (Ursus americanus)

There are some twenty recognized subspecies of black bear, but most are similar enough to make the differences between them of academic importance only. Northern British Columbia is the home of U. a. kermodei—the Kermode bear—which is gray-white, and of U. a. emmonsii—the Glacier bear—which is bluish in color and occurs also in southern Alaska. Apart from these two, there are black bears, ranging in color from jet black to honey blond, from central Mexico to the northern tip of Alaska, and from the Atlantic to the Pacific. In the eastern part of North America, most are black, usually with a tan or grizzled snout and often with a white chest blaze.

They are much smaller than *U. arctos*—the brown or grizzly bear—with weights usually between 200 and 400 lb (90 and 180 kg). They can be very much larger; in 1885, a Wisconsin bear was weighed at 802 lb (364 kg), and nearly seventy years later, in 1953, another Wisconsin bear had a dressed weight of 585 lb (265 kg), representing a live weight of 735 lb (333 kg). On its skull measurement, it is the biggest black bear trophy on record.

Black bears thrive in heavy brushwood and mixed deciduous and coniferous forests, and they are omnivorous, eating whatever they can get. This includes all sorts of vegetable and animal food, and the gleanings of garbage dumps and edibles in hunting cabins and tents. When hungry, black bears are recklessly intrusive and very dangerous, and, at all times of year, they are unpredictable.

There was still a bounty for killing bears in the 1950s, but they are now accorded the status of game animals, and so, bear hunting is regulated. They are protected in national parks, and elsewhere may not be hunted over carrion bait nor, in many regions of the United States, may they be tracked with dogs.

Like *U. arctos*, black bears do not hibernate entirely but seek dens in fall or early winter. A sow either gives birth to cubs in the den, usually in January or February, or has the previous year's cubs with her; in either event, she is unlikely to sleep undisturbed. Both boars and sows are sometimes found in the vicinity of their dens, even in the middle of winter. The length of their usage of dens depends on the local availability of vegetation to eat, so that in the south of their range, where the growing period is long, bears scarcely use a den at all, while in the north they may be in it for more than six months a year.

A usual litter is two cubs, but more occur; a litter of six was observed in 1947, but this must be exceptional. The cubs weigh about ½ lb (225 g) at birth but weigh about 75 lb (34 kg) at the end of their first year. They are usually driven off during their second year, become sexually active at three or four years of age, are full-grown by seven, and may live to thirty. [GG]

Polar Bear *(Ursus maritimus)*

The polar bear is a magnificent animal of the snow, ice, and water of the Arctic. Apart from man, the polar bear's only enemy is the killer whale, which occasionally takes a polar bear.

Polar bears are circumpolar, being found around the entire fringe of the Arctic. This includes the whole arctic coastline of North America, Greenland, and the arctic islands. Bears sometimes wander as far south as James Bay, at the south of Hudson Bay in Canada.

Polar bears are, on average, the largest bears of North America, being generally larger than the brown bears of the northwest Pacific coast. Polar bears weighing over 1,600 lb (725 kg) have been shot, although the average is around 1,000 lb (450 kg). The sows are slightly smaller. The polar bear's color is yellowish-white, and its body is somewhat pear-shaped, for ease in swimming.

Like all bears, polar bears are solitary, although the sows and their partly grown cubs travel together, but once the cubs reach sub-adulthood, they must cope on their own. The only time polar bears are sociable is during their breeding season, which lasts for a short time in early summer. They are polygamous.

Cubs are born after a gestation period of about 240 days. The sows give birth in a den found, perhaps, among jumbles of pressure ice; the cubs are seemingly very small, weighing only about 2 lb (1 kg), or about 0.2 percent of their mature weight. They begin to travel with their mother a few months after they are born and remain with her for two years.

Polar bears eat mostly meat, seal being the main quarry, which the bears can stalk with great skill. They can wait for hours at a breathing

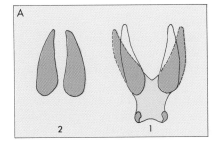

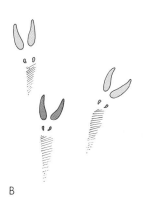

(Opposite) **ALPINE IBEX** (*Capra ibex*).

Above) **CHAMOIS** (*Rupicapra rupicapra*).

The hind (*1*) and fore (*2*) hoof of the ibex. The dashed lines show how the hooves spread to grip when the animal is climbing.
B The ibex's tracks when it is moving at speed.

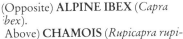

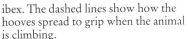

hole to claw out an unwary seal, much as a domestic cat claws out field mice. They eat carrion, too, such as the carcasses of beached whales, and will remain in the vicinity until the meat is consumed. They will eat fish, particularly spawning char and salmon, and will take ground-nesting birds and their eggs, lemmings, and even mice. They have been known to kill musk-ox and walrus, but walrus can put up a formidable resistance.

The United States Marine Mammal Protection Act protects the polar bear from being hunted in the territories of the United States, the only exception being native peoples—i.e., American Indians and Eskimos—who, if they still live in their traditional ways, may hunt polar bears. [JK]

Cottontail Rabbits *(Sylvilagus)*

Cottontail rabbits are among the most popular game animals in North America, not least because they are at home in many different habitats; farms and farm-edges are favorites, in addition to woodlots, old grown-up fields, brushy cutovers, and even swamps. Except for the Pacific coast and the northern parts of New England, they are found everywhere in the United States.

While the common, or eastern, cottontail inhabits most of this range, three subspecies occur in parts of it. The mountain cottontail (*S. nuttalli*) predominates in the Rocky Mountains region, the desert cottontail (*S. auduboni*) predominates in the more arid regions of the West, and the New England cottontail (*S. transitionalis*) predominates through the Appalachians and southern New England.

The eastern cottontail is about 17 inches (43 cm) long and weighs up to a maximum of about 4 lb (1.8 kg). It is brownish-gray, whereas the

mountain and desert cottontails are yellowish, and the New England cottontail is reddish-gray, with a vague blackish patch between ears, during the hunting season. The tail, which appears white and cottony when the animal runs, has given a name to the species.

The eastern cottontail is normally most active early in the morning and late in the evening; when subjected to heavy hunting, it may become nocturnal. It does not dig burrows but makes use of holes dug by woodchucks. Like hares, cottontails tend to circle back to their territory when pursued; the New England cottontail tends to describe larger circles than the eastern. [NS]

Swamp Rabbit *(Sylvilagus aquaticus)*

Swamp Rabbits can weigh up to 6 lb (2.6 kg) and are found in the southern states of the central United States in swamps and marshes. Their hair is coarser than that of the cottontail, and the characteristic nape patch is dark and distinct.

When bolted by hounds, swamp rabbits run in wide circles and do not seek shelter underground, but will swim if pressed. They are plentiful in south-central Tennessee, and chases can last up to an hour, for this rabbit seems to know how to avoid detection and can creep through thick undergrowth when in the vicinity of a hunter. [NS]

Hares *(Lepus)*

A number of hares are found in North America, but not all of them are called hares. The whitetail jackrabbit (*L. townsendii*), which inhabits the northern Rocky Mountains and Great Plains, is one of them; another is

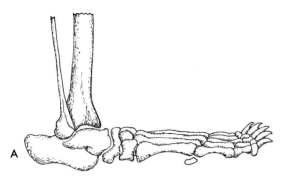

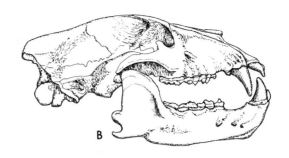

(Left) **POLAR BEAR** (*Ursus maritimus*).
(Below) **BROWN, or GRIZZLY, BEAR** (*Ursus arctos*).
A The bones of the foot of a black bear. The animal walks on the sole of the foot.
B The skull of a brown bear, showing the prominent canine and molar teeth.
C The track of a brown bear; the larger imprints are those of the hind feet.

the blacktail jackrabbit (*L. californicus*), which inhabits the southern part of the Rockies and the Plains. The arctic hare (*L. arcticus*), the tundra hare (*L. othus*), and the snowshoe, or varying, hare (*L. americanus*) are other species. The snowshoe is found across the northern part of the United States, well south through the Rocky Mountains in the West and in the Appalachians in the East, and over almost all of Canada. The tundra hare inhabits the tundra coastal region of Alaska.

All hares have long ears and very long back legs, hear and see excellently, and can run fast and with stamina, preferring to run uphill when pursued or in danger. Being strongly territorial, hares run in a wide circle when hunted by dogs, and will eventually try to return to their own familiar area. They live above ground and, unlike rabbits, do not seek shelter in holes.

Both the tundra and the snowshoe have coats that change from brown in summer to white in winter. The whitetail jackrabbit may change its coat in the northern part of its range, but the blacktail jackrabbit does not. [NS]

Brown Hare *(Lepus europaeus)*

This is the most hunted, but not the only, hare in Europe. The Alpine hare (*L. timidus*) inhabits the Alps and the Scandinavian mountains, and a subspecies occurs in Scotland, where it is called the blue hare (*L. t. scoticus*), for, in spring and fall, its coat has a bluish cast because the brown fur of summer is mingled with the white hairs of winter. Smaller than the brown hare, with longer legs and longer ears, it prefers high, rocky terrain. Ireland has its own subspecies, the Irish hare (*L. t. hibernicus*), which looks like the blue hare but has a proportionately larger head and shorter ears; it does not turn white as regularly as the blue hare, and its winter coat is often white patched with russet. In general, though, the brown hare has a white coat in winter.

Regional variations occur, the British subspecies being darker brown than the hares on the continent of Europe, while there are slight differences in average size, with hares from the north being generally larger than those from the south.

The continents of Asia and Africa have each their local race and,

together, some seven subspecies, each more or less resembling the brown hare, but differing in details such as skull structure.

The brown hare has been transplanted to North America, where it now ranges from the Great Lakes region through much of the State of New York and into western New England. It overlaps with the cottontail rabbit and the snowshoe hare.

The brown hare has an average length of about 25 inches (64 cm) and an average weight of about 9 lb (4 kg). It is a close relative of the North American jackrabbit, which is a hare, and not a rabbit, despite its name.

Brown hare live above ground, out in the open at all times of year. They rely on their ability to detect visible or audible danger, and to hide or to run so as to escape it: their sight and hearing are excellent, they can crouch down and become all but invisible but, when they run, they run extremely fast and strongly, preferring to run uphill, when their long, powerful back legs are of great advantage. Their numbers can be considerable, so much so as to constitute a menace to crops: perhaps, on good agricultural land, in excess of one hare to every 3 acres (1 hectare).

Hares form an important link in the food chain, for foxes, the larger hawks and eagles, and other predators depend on them for their own survival. [TT]

(Above) **SNOWSHOE HARE** (*Lepus americanus*).
(Left) **BROWN HARE** (*Lepus europaeus*).

(Below) **COTTONTAIL RABBIT** (*Sylvilagus*).

Gray Fox (*Urocyon cinereoargentatus*)

The gray fox is indigenous only to North America, chiefly to the eastern United States. It is the same size as the red fox but not usually as luxuriously furred. Its color is mostly peppery gray, but with some rust, white underparts, and a black brush tip.

It is hunted by the same methods as the red fox (see below). Unlike the red, it uses dens in winter—most often in rocky crevices or other hollows in sloping woodlands. It is more shy of open fields than the red fox. At one time, ferrets were sometimes used (as they have been used to hunt European red foxes) to move them from their dens. In the United States, ferreting is generally illegal, but small dogs are used for the same purpose by a few hunters. This is not, however, a common method.

When pursued by hounds, the gray fox is neither as fast nor as long-running as the red fox, for it has smaller lungs and slightly shorter legs. However, it provides good sport, and good practice for hounds. When tracked without hounds or enticed by a predator call, it is as canny and difficult to take as the red fox. Moreover, it has a unique ability that it exhibits when pursued. It can climb trees. The only American canine species with real tree-climbing ability, it readily scrambles up a leaning or thickly branched tree when pressed, or it eludes hounds and hunter by plunging into very thick, tangled cover and then "holing," climbing, backtracking, or employing some other maneuver to lose its pursuers. [RE]

Red Fox (*Vulpes fulva*)

At one time, the Eurasian and North American red foxes were thought to be separate species, but they are one and the same. In North America alone, there are probably a dozen subspecies of red fox, the number being uncertain because of range overlap, interbreeding, and color and size variations that do not qualify local populations for the status of a distinct race. Additional subspecies inhabit virtually all of Europe and much of Asia and Africa.

In the British Isles and Continental Europe, the typical hunter who carries a gun may shoot any fox he encounters as vermin—a game- and poultry-destroying pest. In that part of the world (indeed, in most parts) the red fox is not considered game by riflemen or shotgunners. It is game only for those equestrian sportsmen who ride to hounds. In North America, however, it is shot as game, and in many regions has legal game status—with seasons and limits. Wildlife managers in the United States, though they are not equally progressive with regard to all species, have

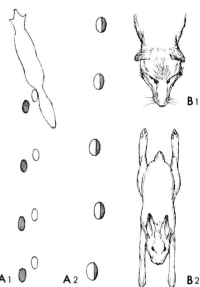

A₁   A₂   B₁   B₂

proved that the fox rarely causes any serious depletion of poultry or other farm stock and is not detrimental to rabbits, ground-nesting game birds, or other wildlife populations if its own population is kept in balance.

An average adult red fox weighs no more than 7 to 12 lb (3 to 7 kg). Its fur makes it look bigger, but it is the size of a house cat or small dog. Its color is generally coppery or rusty, with some peppering, white underparts, and black feet, but there are wide variations. The tip of the copiously furred tail, or brush, is white. America has another important species, the gray fox, and some color variations of the two species can cause confusion, but a white tail tip always marks the red fox. That of the gray fox is always black.

Red foxes den for whelping and rearing their young but, unlike grays, they do not normally den for shelter in the winter. They like mixed, brushy habitat and fields where they can have a good view of potential enemies and good hunting for rodents, rabbits, and other small prey.

The traditional American method of hunting them is with hounds. Sometimes, the hunters take all their enjoyment from watching or hearing their dogs work and do not bother to shoot the quarry. Sometimes, however, they try to intercept the line of chase or wait at likely openings and crossings in the cover, using shotguns to kill the fast-fleeing fox. A second method, which employs smallbore centerfire rifles more often than shotguns, is to track and scout for foxes on snow, without the aid of hounds. A red fox generally naps after mousing or taking other game. He is likely to do so on a small hummock or rise with a good view. He curls up but faces his back trail and frequently raises his head to look for danger. He does not sleep soundly but only "cat-naps." Getting within range and getting a clear shot before the fox detects intrusion and escapes is therefore a challenging sport.

Another method, and one steadily increasing in popularity, is to conceal oneself and attract a fox within rifle or shotgun range by sounding a predator call. In some states, phonographic calls are legal for predators (including not only fox but bobcat, coyote, raccoon, and cougar), but a mouth-blown call is more challenging. Its sound usually imitates the squeal of an injured or terrified rabbit. Some predator calls mimic the sounds of injured birds or other creatures. [RE]

Gray Squirrel (*Sciurus carolinensis*)

The gray squirrel is one of the most sought-after game animals in North America. The species ranges through the United States and southern Canada from the middle of the Great Plains eastward to the Atlantic Ocean. The western gray squirrel (*S. griseus*) is found from the nut groves of southern California to the slopes of Mount Rainier in Washington.

Gray squirrels weigh on average about 1 lb (0.5 kg), but older animals can weigh fifty percent more. Their tails are long and bushy, hence their common name of "bushytail." They are a grizzled gray with a whitish underside. They inhabit large woods, especially those containing trees producing ample supplies of acorns, beechmast, hickory nuts, hazelnuts, and walnuts. In the south, they eat pecans, and, in the west, almonds. If such foods are scarce, gray squirrels will also eat corn. [NS]

Fox Squirrel (*Sciurus niger*)

This squirrel is found in the same parts of the United States and Canada as the gray, with the exception of New England, where it is seldom seen. It is slightly bigger than the gray, with an average weight of 1½ lb (0.65 kg), and up to 3 lb (1.3 kg) for older animals.

It is a rusty yellow with some gray markings and has an orange belly. In some parts of its range—especially in the Carolinas—it is typically black with white facial markings.

The fox squirrel is at home in woodlots where mast- and nut-producing trees are close to farm-field openings. It often ventures into grain fields, eating especially corn. [NS]

Raccoon (Procyon lotor)

The raccoon is a grayish-brown, thick-furred nocturnal carnivore with a bushy, ring-marked tail, and a characteristically masked face. Raccoons weigh between about 12 and 35 lb (5.4 and 15.9 kg) as adults and can weigh even more. They are found near water all over North and Central America in wooded areas (but not in the Rocky Mountains), where they survive by eating omnivorously.

Related to the panda, raccoons, including here the coati species of the southwestern United States and Central and South America, are agile and climb trees easily, which is how most raccoon hunts end, with the animal "treed." Like foxes, they are intelligent, if not so fast over the ground. They can also swim; in water, a large raccoon is a match for a hound and can even kill it. [NS]

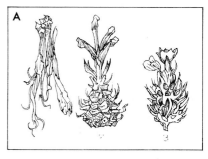

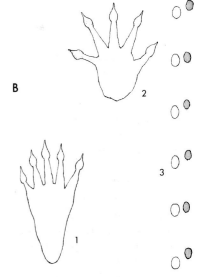

(Top) **GRAY SQUIRREL** (*Sciurus carolinensis*).
(Left) **RACCOON** (*Procyon lotor*).
A Signs that squirrels have been feeding. (*1*) Remains of an unripe pine cone. (*2*) Remains of a ripe cone. (*3*) Remains of a larch cone.
B The raccoon's rear footprint (*1*), front footprint (*2*), and tracks (*3*).

47

(Above) **EURASIAN WOOD-COCK** (*Scolopax rusticola*).
(Left) **COMMON SNIPE** (*Gallinago gallinago*).

A

A Snipe "drum" as their outer tail feathers vibrate during their mating display.
B Woodcock have eyes so placed as to give binocular backward vision, a vital facility when the bird is probing in deep, soft soil.

Chapter 2
Upland Fowl

Eurasian Woodcock *(Scolopax rusticola)*

The Eurasian, or European, woodcock is closely related to the American variety and resembles it closely, but it is a bit bigger—13 to 14 inches (33 to 36 cm) as against 10 to 12 inches (25 to 30 cm). Its bill is proportionately bigger, too. Close relatives of snipe, but rounder in the body, both species of woodcock belong to the sandpiper family, being essentially long-legged small shorebirds that have some characteristics in common with upland birds.

They like moist habitat, however, though not so boggy as that favored by snipe, for they probe for earthworms, which are their principal food, as well as for grubs and insects. They are found in wet deciduous, coniferous, or mixed woodlands, scrub, and even on the edges of moorland, where they may occur together with grouse. Their chalky-white droppings, and the round holes caused by their probing for food, indicate their presence.

Their coloration is generally dark, while their underparts are barred with light and dark brown. Their legs and bills are a dull fleshy or fleshy-gray color. Their wings are rounded, and their large eyes are set far back in the head.

They are crepuscular. At dawn and dusk, they fly in courtship displays that are known, in Britain, as roding. A roding woodcock flies a regular course at 20 to 30 feet (6 to 9 m) with slow, owlish wingbeats, usually at sunset, sometimes in the early morning. Roding may last an hour. Since a roding male is indicating his territory, other woodcock will be chased away; especially during roding, the male may utter a high-pitched sneezing cry or a croak that may be produced by a rush of air through the primaries. Woodcock have a fairly elaborate courtship display, which takes place as early as March (in the southern part of their range, which borders on the Mediterranean countries). A hen with a brood of young will feign injury if disturbed; woodcock have often been observed to carry their chicks from one place to another, by flying for short distances with them usually between their feet.

They hold tight for pointing dogs, and they will usually let a flushing dog approach quite close before flushing into the air; they may, however, scurry or skulk off through ground cover before rising. Cocker spaniels got their name from their use in flushing woodcock.

Their range is extensive, stretching across Europe eastward from the British Isles, excluding only the sub-Arctic north and the dry Mediterranean region, through the whole of Asia to Japan. [RE]

American Woodcock *(Philohela minor)*

Despite the total difference of their Latin names, the American and the Eurasian woodcock are essentially the same species in general appearance and habits. A dark, plump bird of wet and swampy woods, with rounded wings, an extremely long bill, and capable of producing a whistling noise in flight (made by the action of its wings), the American woodcock has spread in recent years from the Maritime Provinces of Canada as far away as the American Midwest.

The woodcock's presence may be detected by the round drill holes it leaves in soft ground, in which it probes for earthworms, its principal food, and by the chalky-white splashes of its droppings, which are a more noticeable sign. The woodcock is migratory, being forced to move when the first frosts harden the ground, but it is a species that returns unerringly to the same fields on its return migration.

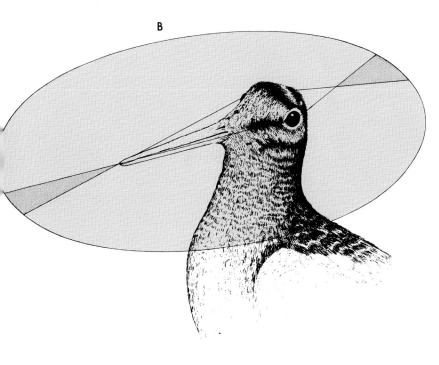

B

(Below) **CALIFORNIA QUAIL**
(*Lophortyx californicus*).
(Opposite, top) **BOBWHITE
QUAIL** (*Colinus virginanus*).
(Opposite, lower) **SCALED QUAIL**
(*Callipepla squamata*).
A Only one species of North American quail has a long, erect head plume: the mountain quail (*Oreortyx pictus*).
B Two North American species of quail have rounded, forward-inclining plumes, and, of these, one has a distinctive black patch on its belly: Gambel's quail (*Lophortyx gambelii*).
**C MEARNS', or HARLEQUIN,
QUAIL** (*Cyrtonyx montezumae*).

A   B   C

Breeding is preceded by an elaborate courting ritual in which the male flies vertically up from the ground, uttering a sound that can be represented as a deep, guttural "peent." The ritual takes place at dawn or dusk, and the bird can disappear in the dim light, only to descend again, uttering the same cry. This can continue for twenty to thirty minutes.

Woodcock are now found over the entire eastern United States, plus southern Ontario, Quebec, and the Maritime Provinces. They generally nest from Pennsylvania and Ohio northward to the limits of their range; they winter mainly along the delta of the Mississippi and elsewhere in the Deep South. [NS]

Common Snipe *(Capella gallinago* or *Gallinago gallinago)*

There are large numbers of species and subspecies of snipe in various parts of the world, where there exist the marshes and bogs that provide the right environmental conditions. The various species encompass several genera, but all belong to the family of wading birds, the *Scolopacidae,* and all have similar habits.

Some—the European jack snipe, for example—are smaller than the common snipe; some—the great snipe of Scandinavia and northeastern Europe is one—are larger. The New Zealand snipe has the odd habit of nesting in the deserted underground burrows of other birds, whereas all other snipe nest above ground, employing a grass-lined hollow. The great snipe is alone in having a communal courtship display. Whatever its Latin or common name, it is probably safe to say that—to a hunter—a snipe is a snipe, and that a description of the common snipe will suffice for all.

This bird looks rather like the woodcock but is smaller and not so bulky. It is usually about 10½ inches (27 cm) long, with long legs and a long, slender bill. It has mottled brown plumage, horizontally barred with black, and it has black stripes through the eyes.

As with those of woodcock, snipe droppings look like chalky spatters on the ground, while the snipe's feeding habits of probing in soft ground leave round holes. Snipe feed in boggier ground, however, and rely less on earthworms than do woodcock.

Snipe are difficult to observe on the ground, but they can be flushed from marsh plants such as sedges and bullrushes, when they will rise with their characteristic zigzag flight and hoarse cry. Their flight straightens after some 30 feet (9 m), a fact well known to experienced hunters, who prefer to wait out their snipe before firing. Snipe fly into the wind and generally return to the spot from which they were flushed. [RE]

Wilson's Snipe *(Capella gallinago delicata)*

When flushed, this American snipe, like snipe elsewhere in the world, flies in a characteristic zigzag and is, therefore, a challenge for even an expert shot. It is called jack or common snipe in North America, but these are the names of two separate species in Europe; *Lymnocryptes minima* and *Gallinago gallinago.* It is very slightly smaller than the American woodcock, which flies straighter when flushed, and has rounded wings, not pointed ones. In addition, the woodcock inhabits swampy woody ground, whereas the Wilson's snipe is found in open swamps, bogs, boggy meadows, and pastures.

Within North America, this snipe breeds all across Canada and over much of the northern United States, and winters practically anywhere in the United States and northern Mexico where the terrain is suitable; some snipe migrate further south, reaching as far as Brazil. [NS]

Bobwhite Quail *(Colinus virginianus)*

This is the classic bird of American upland hunting. Small grain fields and wide fencerows maintained large populations of bobwhites, but this type of agriculture has given way to one demanding huge open fields. Some landowners have, however, continued to manage their land with an eye to hunting bobwhites, and the birds also occur on some state-owned lands managed with the purpose of keeping up populations of these and other upland birds.

These quail are small (8½ to 10½ inches/22 to 27 cm) and generally brownish with light and dark reddish tints in some feathers. They gather in bevies of a dozen up to thirty. [NS]

Scaled Quail *(Callipepla squamata)*

This quail is indigenous to the arid country of western Texas, New Mexico, southeastern Arizona, and Mexico.

Its breast feathers have the appearance of scales and give the bird its name. Its back is gray, and its upper back, upper breast, and neck have a bluish cast. Both males and females have a white, cottony crest, which is more pronounced on males. The bird is also known as the "cottontop" and as the blue quail.

These quail gather in bevies of up to one hundred birds, but most commonly, numbers in a bevy do not exceed twenty. They run rather than fly, unless forcefully flushed. [NS]

Gambel's Quail *(Lophortyx gambelii)*

Gambel's quail, like the scaled, prefers dry country and occurs in Arizona, western New Mexico, southern California, and in Mexico south of the Arizona border, but less profusely there than in the United States.

This quail and the California quail have a black head plume that bends forward; the mountain quail also has a black head plume, but it is upright. The Gambel's is distinguished from the California by a black belly spot; otherwise, the two species are similar, with faces and necks outlined in white, reddish crowns, chestnut sides, and brownish backs. Like scaled quail, Gambel's prefer to run before they fly. [NS]

California Quail *(Lophortyx californicus)*

This quail occurs on the west coast of the United States, from southern California to Washington. It prefers mixed woodlands in valleys and foothills but will move onto farmland and has been known to gorge on grapes in the wine country in California.

The males of the species are similar to those of the Gambel's quail. The females are also similar, but the California hen has a light throat.

California quail sometimes flock together in huge bevies, but most contain about twenty-five to sixty birds. Several such bevies may be found close to one another. Like most quail, this one runs strongly before it flies.

The species is also known as the valley quail, to differentiate it from the mountain quail. [NS]

Mountain Quail *(Oreortyx pictus)*

This quail occurs in the same geographical regions as the California, or valley, quail but is found most commonly in the mountainous regions and chaparral, often adjoining small streams. It can be distinguished from the California quail by its long straight head plume, and by white bars on its sides. The sexes are similar, although the female is duller in color.

Like other quail, the mountain quail runs strongly and is reluctant to fly; it must, therefore, be flushed vigorously if the hunter is to get a shot at it in the air. [NS]

Mearns', or Harlequin, Quail *(Cyrtonyx montezumae)*

This is a bird of the mountainous country between 4,000 and 6,000 feet (1,200 and 1,800 m) in southeastern Arizona in the United States and in the states of Chihuahua, Coahuila, and Sonora in Mexico.

It has a plump shape and is slightly smaller than the other quail noted here. Its second name is derived from the black and white pattern of the feathers on its face; the females are brownish, while the males are more a reddish-gray.

This quail, like all the others of the arid regions of North America, fluctuates in numbers in proportion to the annual rainfall. [NS]

Crested Quail *(Colinus cristatus)*

This is the quail of northern South America and is especially prevalent in Columbia. Its crest is similar to that of American plumed quail but, when pointed by a dog, it does not flush wildly as they do, but sits tightly, hiding like the bobwhite and the Mearns' quail. It flocks in coveys and occurs around cattle pastures; it eats principally weed seeds. [NS]

Chachalaca *(Ortalis vetula)*

This is an unusual game bird of northeastern Mexico, found around openings in woodlands and thickets. Its name derives from its loud raucous call. It is about 20 to 24 inches (51 to 61 cm) long.

It has a long tail and a small head. Its general coloration is brownish, but the tail, which is rounded and tipped with white, has a greenish sheen. [NS]

Wild Turkey *(Meleagris gallopavo)*

There are at least half a dozen subspecies of the wild turkey which, itself, looks very much like a slim version of the farmyard bird. The males are much larger than the females and have more intensely colored red wattles. All mature males and—confusingly—some females develop "beards" comprised of a hanging tuft of feathers on the breast.

Of the subspecies, the eastern is the most numerous, having been introduced most successfully throughout the east, south, and midwest of the United States, after a period of continuous decline caused by the felling of the forests that had been the turkey's natural habitat. The rehabilitation of the wild turkey is one of the big success stories of North American game preservation.

The bird needs mature forests providing acorns, walnuts, hickory nuts, hazelnuts, beechmast, and the like, especially in winter when abundant food is essential to its survival.

Turkeys roost in trees, staying in the same place all night. They are very wary and have good eyesight, and are thus difficult to approach.

All the subspecies have essentially the same general form as the principal species, but they vary in size and, to some degree, in coloration, too. Starting with the largest, the Florida, or osceola, turkey can weigh up to 22 lb (10 kg) and is found chiefly in central Florida, but it can occur further north, where intergrading may occur; it is lighter than the eastern turkey. The Merriam turkey is close in size and appearance to the eastern turkey, and it is, in effect, the wild turkey of the Rocky Mountains region, occurring in large numbers in Colorado, Arizona, parts of New Mexico, and in California, Wyoming, Montana, and parts of some other western states. The Rio Grande turkey is smaller, weighing about 10 lb (4 kg) on average and is relatively pale; it is a native of Mexico and the lower southwestern United States and has been successfully introduced into Oklahoma and Kansas. Gould's turkey and the Mexican turkey are so much alike that there is disagreement as to whether or not they are separate subspecies; they are small, leggy birds, but, despite this, they are the ancestors of the now much larger domestic turkey. Finally, the ocellated turkey of the jungles of Central America and the Yucatan Peninsula in Mexico: it is slightly smaller than the eastern and Merriam turkeys, and is a separate species *(Agriocharis ocellata)*. [NS]

Tinamous *(Tinamidae)*

There are at least forty-five different species of tinamous, a family of Central and South American birds, of which most are jungle birds and,

(Left) **WILD TURKEY** (*Meleagris gallopavo*).
(Above) **CHACHALACA** (*Ortalis vetula*).
(Center) The wild turkey in flight.

therefore, seldom hunted; only a few species—those found principally on the pampas of Uruguay and Argentina, and one on the plateaux of Ecuador—are frequently shot.

Tinamous vary in size, with the larger species being about the size of a cock pheasant and the smaller about that of a partridge. Their general form is rounded, with a very short tail almost completely covered by the wings when they are folded; the head and neck are slender, the beak is down-curving. Their legs are strong, being typical of a bird that spends much time on the ground.

Remarkable in a number of respects, tinamous are perhaps strangest in that only the male birds incubate the eggs. The females, moreover, usually lay two or three eggs in each of a number of nests. The eggs themselves are all manner of colors: green, turquoise, purple, wine-red, chocolate, slate-gray, even black. The young are precocious, being ready to feed with the parent birds almost immediately after hatching; the eggs are, significantly, exceptionally large, at least in some species, weighing up to ten or eleven percent of the weight of the hen bird.

On the pampas, the hunter can expect to encounter three species, the spotted, the martineta, or crested, and the red-winged tinamous, respectively *Nothura maculosa*, *Eudromia elegans*, and *Rhynchotus rufescens*. The spotted is the most abundant and is about the size of a partridge. The martineta is a beautiful pheasant-sized bird with black and white barred feathers (excellent for trout flies), and a long, slender crest on its head. The red-winged, named for its characteristic appearance, is scarce compared with either of the other two species and is wary, flushing usually at nearly maximum shotgun range on almost every encounter. Its local name is *perdiz colorado*.

Both the spotted and the martineta are found in coveys, but do not flush together; the martineta, particularly, flushes one at a time, giving the hunter little time to reload when the covey numbers ten or twelve birds. When flushed, they fly like pheasants, with furious wing beats followed by glides. Although shooting is sporting, in the almost total absence of cover—which must be seen to be believed—it is nowhere as difficult as with grouse or woodcock.

Shooting in Ecuador is quite another matter, for the birds, of the genus *Nothoprocta* and called partridge tinamous, are at home on the high plateaux of the Andes, at 10,000 to 12,000 feet (3,000 to 4,000 m); the hunter, and his dogs, must accustom themselves to these conditions. These birds are hardly gregarious, like the tinamous of the pampas, and usually flush one at a time. [AL & NS]

(Above left) **TINAMOUS** (*Nothura maculosa*).
(Above) **MOURNING DOVE** (*Zenaidura macroura*).
(Opposite, above) **ROCK DOVE, or DOMESTIC PIGEON** (*Columba livia*).

PIGEONS AND DOVES

These names are confusingly interchangeable, particularly when it is remembered that, in Britain, doves are protected while the woodpigeon (*Columba palumbus*) is not and may, therefore, be shot as a pest. *Columba livia* is called either rock dove or domestic pigeon in North America, but rock dove in Britain.

Rock Dove, or Domestic Pigeon *(Columbia livia)*

This bird is very common in practically every urban area of the United States; in Europe, it occurs only in the Mediterranean countries and round the coasts of Scotland and Ireland.

It has a white patch at the base of the tail, two dark stripes on its wings, and a dark band on its tail. The British woodpigeon, *Columba palumbus*, is larger and has a conspicuous white marking on its neck and on the wings. When they fly up in alarm, both species make a loud clapping noise, caused by their wings striking together.

C. livia is a hardy bird, perhaps because it rarely has trouble in finding food. It is tame in the parks and city squares of North America, but it is very wary in the countryside, where it is regarded as a pest. [NS]

Scaled Pigeon *(Columbigallina passerina)*

This is a small, fast-flying bird found in many areas, but perhaps most in the mountains of Central and northern South America. Its name derives from the appearance of its breast feathers; the scaled quail is so named for the same reason. [NS]

Band-tailed Pigeon *(Columba fasciata)*

This bird summers in the mountains of Nicaragua, Costa Rica, and northern Panama, and migrates northward to breed in northern Mexico, New Mexico, Texas, Arizona, and parts of Colorado, and along the coast of California, and even of Oregon and Washington.

Slightly bigger than a rock dove, the band-tailed pigeon gets its name from the gray band on its broad tail. Other distinguishing features include a bright yellow bill, bright yellow feet, and a semi-circular white ring on the nape of its neck. It flies fast and uses thermal air currents.

In the Central American mountains, the band-tailed pigeon feeds mainly on a grape-like berry that abounds in the trees that shade the coffee plantations.[NS]

White-crowned Pigeon *(Columba leucocephala)*

This American bird gets its name from its shining white crown, for it is otherwise completely dark. It nests in the Florida Keys and often migrates to Cuba during the summer. It used to be hunted there, before the Revolution, and may one day be accessible again to visiting hunters. [NS]

Sand-grouse *(Pteroclidae)*

This family of birds includes several species, but they are pigeons, despite a number of resemblances to grouse. For example, they have short, feathered legs, grouse-like beaks, stout bodies, nest on the ground, and do not perch. Like pigeons, however, they lay few eggs per clutch, and their young are precocious and fast-growing. Sand-grouse look like doves in flight and are about the same size as a rock dove, but their coloration is like that of a partridge.

They like dry desert country and so occur rarely in Europe but more commonly in Africa, Asia Minor, Asia proper, and parts of India. They feed on seeds and fruit, and the birds can often be observed flying down to water-holes, for example in safari-country in Africa. [NS]

Mourning Dove *(Zenaidura macroura)*

This dove nests in eastern Canada, the eastern United States, and even in Mexico; it migrates to the south of its nesting grounds, and so can be found in the eastern United States for most of the year. It is a common species, being smaller and slimmer than the domestic pigeon (or rock dove), and with a brownish or grayish coloration and a pointed tail. The mourning dove flies fast but can change direction easily. In some of the

(Top) **VARIEGATED SAND-GROUSE** *(Pterocles burchelli).*
(Center) **WHITE-WINGED DOVE** *(Zenaida asiatica).*
(Right) **CHESTNUT-BELLIED SAND-GROUSE** *(Pterocles exustus).*

states it is classified as a song bird, and protected accordingly; not entirely paradoxically, the states in which it enjoys most protection are those in which it is scarcest.

Mourning doves flock together, often to grain fields after the harvest. Modern agricultural machinery leaves plenty of gleanings behind and the doves gorge themselves. They can do some crop damage, too, but this can be kept down by shooting. There seems to be little pattern to their migration, perhaps because—according to estimates—the annual mortality of this species is sixty to eighty percent. [NS]

White-winged Dove *(Zenaida asiatica)*

This dove is just about the same size as the mourning dove (11 to 12 inches/28 to 30 cm) but has conspicuous white patches on its wings. Its tail is rounded and has white "corners." Like most doves, it is a strong flier. It has a strong, rather owlish call note that contrasts with the melancholy call of the mourning dove and the purring coo of the European turtle dove.

White-wings tolerate, or even favor, more arid climes than those that suit the mourning dove, but in other respects their habitats are similar. Like all doves, the white-wing thrives in good agricultural land and

seems to do especially well in farm country that has been newly converted to small grain crops. This has been observed on the west coast of Mexico, where irrigation has caused the former desert to bloom, and in the Mexican state of Campeche, in southwestern Yucatan, where the jungle has been cut and replaced by rice fields.

White-wings and mourning doves occur together in southwestern Texas and northeastern Mexico, and on some Caribbean islands, notably Cuba. The white-winged dove's nesting range in the United States includes southwest Texas, southern New Mexico, Arizona, and California; it nests in northern Mexico, too. It is hunted in these states, and the other areas mentioned, and in a number of central American countries—Guatemala, Honduras, El Salvador, Nicaragua, Costa Rica, and Panama—to which it migrates. It only sometimes reaches as far south as Panama, doing so only when food is scarce in countries further to the north. [NS]

Columbian, or White-tailed, Dove *(Zenaida auriculata caucae)*

This dove looks very much like the mourning dove but has perhaps more white in its tail, which is shorter and less pointed. Also, the white-tail has

dark iridescent blue, rather than black, facial markings. A similar species, found in the West Indies, lacks the white tail markings; it is sometimes called the eared dove.

There are some white-tailed doves in Panama, but they are overwhelmingly abundant in Columbia. They nest all the year round, but with a concentration into three major breeding periods. The young birds are sexually mature at the age of four months.

A further factor that has contributed to the enormous numbers of white-tails is the change in farming methods in Columbia. The jungles have been cut, and farmland has been given over to small grains—rice, wheat, and sorghum. The doves feed on these, being estimated to consume about twenty percent of the entire crop, and glean the fields in the fifteen-day period between harvest and replanting. The birds have become a major pest, and hunting is unrestricted. [NS]

Ptarmigan (Lagopus)

This family of birds is circumpolar in range, occurring on the Arctic tundra of North America, Greenland, Iceland, the Scandinavian mountains, and Siberia. Their southern limits in North America extend to British Columbia and the Rockies, northern Minnesota, Maine, and the Adirondack Mountains of New York State. In Europe, ptarmigan are found on the hills of northern Scotland, in the Alps, in the Pyrenees, and in Scandinavia.

Ptarmigan are about the same size as partridge, or a bit bigger. In winter, they are white, with black markings that vary from subspecies to subspecies; in summer, they are generally brown, with white wings. Subspecies overlap in range to some extent, and it can be difficult to distinguish one from another.

In North America, the rock (L. mutus) and willow (L. lagopus) ptarmigan are very similar, for their summer plumage is generally brown with white wings, and their winter plumage white with black tails. The willow is a darker brown in summer, while the rock can be grayish. In winter, the rock has a black streak from the bill, which is smaller and more slender, to the eye. The rock ptarmigan prefers the most exposed and barren hills, while the willow prefers sheltered ground. A third species, the white-tailed ptarmigan (L. leucurus), has a white tail at all times of year.

In Europe, the ptarmigan (L. mutus) is the bird known in North America as the rock ptarmigan. In Scotland, it occurs together with the red grouse (L. l. scoticus), and in Scandinavia with the willow grouse (L. lagopus); these grouse are regarded as conspecific. They are slightly larger than the ptarmigan (15 to 16 inches/38 to 41 cm, as against about

14 inches/36 cm). They differ in appearance from the ptarmigan very much as the North American ptarmigan do from one another. The ptarmigan occupies higher ground than do either of the grouse.

The red grouse is described separately (below). A little confusingly, in the British Isles, ptarmigan are sometimes regarded as species of grouse, whereas the opposite view is generally held elsewhere. A partial explanation may be that the red grouse was known, in Gaelic, as *tármachan*, before it got the name of grouse.

Most ptarmigan and grouse are virtually inaccessible to man during winter, when they live much of the time in burrows and tunnels under the snow. Some are trapped in winter, for example in Swedish Lapland, where winter temperatures can be as low as –40°C (–40°F).

The willow ptarmigan of North America is an exception, for it can be found in winter on the shores of bays and rivers in the more wooded sections of the north. The birds can be seen on the tidal flats, at the high tide mark, and in the stands of small willow and other bushes that afford shelter and food.

Ptarmigan in North America are relatively unwary birds for, where they have not been hunted, they are unafraid of man. For this reason, they are sometimes known as "fool hens," together with western ruffed grouse and spruce grouse. [NK]

Red Grouse *(Lagopus scoticus)*
This is the grouse of the British Isles, where it occurs on the high hills of Scotland, northern England, and Wales. There have been red grouse on high ground in southwestern England, and a small number have been introduced into the Ardennes in Belgium.

They are plump, reddish-brown birds, about 15 to 16 inches (38 to 41 cm) long; in winter, their plumage changes to white and can cause confusion with ptarmigan (see above). They have a loud crowing call and, in the breeding season, a call often rendered as "go-back, go-back, go-back."

They inhabit hills above the treeline. Their principal food is heather which, in Scotland, has traditionally been burned off, in the practice known as "muirburn," which allows young shoots to grow, while fertilizing the ground with ashes. While grouse became of sporting (and commercial) interest in the nineteenth century, sheep have been grazed in the Scottish highlands since at least the eighteenth century. Both eat heather, however, but in Britain of the last quarter of the twentieth century, grouse are perhaps the more valuable of the two animals.

Populations of grouse vary from year to year, depending in part on the weather in spring after eggs have hatched, when the young birds are vulnerable to exceptional wet and cold. Apart from muirburn, grouse can be supported by draining bogs, and by plowing up grit, which these birds eat, as do many grouse and ptarmigan. [NS]

Ruffed Grouse *(Bonasa umbellus)*
This North American grouse is a bird of the briars, brambles, and early new growth that flourishes after woods and forests have been cut. Ruffed grouse are rarely seen on the ground, for they like to stay in thick cover. When they do fly up, it is very suddenly and with an explosive whirring of wings.

The cocks and the hens are about the same size (16 to 19 inches/41 to 50 cm) and with a prominent dark-barred fantail. In the hen, the barring may be broken in the center, whereas that on the cock is unbroken. The birds from the Pacific states are typically reddish-brown, while those from the Rockies are grayish. They have, however, a wide distribution across North America, occurring through most of Canada and the Pacific Northwest, and from the Midwest to the Atlantic: in Minnesota, Wisconsin, Michigan, Ohio, Pennsylvania, New York, all of New England, the Maritime Provinces of Canada, and in Quebec and Ontario.

(Opposite) **WILLOW PTARMIGAN** *(Lagopus lagopus)* in summer plumage.
(Top) **RED GROUSE** *(Lagopus scoticus)*.

(Center) **ROCK PTARMIGAN** *(Lagopus mutus)*.
(Below) The rock ptarmigan in winter plumage.

The male of the species has an identifiable "drumming" display, which produces a characteristic noise like the roll of a drum or a muffled thumping. This is caused by the cock beating its wings fiercely while standing erect, sometimes on an old log or some other low perch. The birds do this most before and during mating, but also at other times of year, if not so frequently.

It has been discovered that ruffed grouse do exceptionally well in aspen woods and forests in which trees are at stages of growth from seedlings up to forty-year-old trees. Timber and wildlife managers have been taking advantage of this; ruffed grouse have responded by developing high populations, using the newly cut areas for cover, nesting in the slightly more developed areas, and feeding on the buds produced by the mature trees. Ruffed grouse lay up to about twenty eggs and are capable of increasing rapidly in population; cold, wet weather after chicks hatch causes a dearth of insects, on which the young feed, and, later, a fall in the overall population. [NS]

Spruce Grouse *(Canachites canadensis)*
This is a bird of the deep wet forests of Canada and Alaska. It is about the same size as the ruffed grouse, darker, and unwary, tending to perch in trees undisturbed by the presence of hunters. This is why it—like the ruffed grouse and ptarmigan in an unhunted area—is known as the "fool hen."

In addition to in Canada and Alaska, it occurs locally in the northern parts of some of the United States: New York, Michigan, and Minnesota. [NS]

Sharptailed Grouse *(Pedioecetes phasianellus)*
This bird's most distinctive feature is its short, pointed tail, which appears white in flight. The sharptailed grouse is distinguished from the prairie chicken (see below), which shares the same habitat of brushland bordering on farmland, by its lack of the prairie chicken's feather tufts, which hang down noticeably on either side of the neck, and by the fact that it does not have the rounded, dark tail of the prairie chicken. The two birds are about the same size (17 to 18 inches/43 to 46 cm).

Sharptailed grouse occur in the upper midwestern United States and in the prairie provinces of Canada. [NS]

Greater Prairie Chicken *(Tympanuchus cupido)*
This North American bird was once plentiful in the extreme, for it

(Opposite) **SPRUCE GROUSE**
(*Canachites canadensis*).
(Left) **SAGE GROUSE** (*Centrocerus urophasianus*).

flourished in the fencerows that were maintained to border grain and pasture fields on the midwestern prairies; these fencerows have been eliminated in the interests of creating larger and larger fields and with them have gone all but relatively few prairie chickens. These are now found together with sharptailed grouse and with the gray or Hungarian partridges that have been introduced into North America.

Prairie chicken have a characteristic group courtship ritual, in which the males produce a hollow booming call, similar to the noise generated by blowing across the top of a bottle.

They are about the same size as the sharptailed grouse and have a short, dark, rounded tail; they are brownish in color. [NS]

Lesser Prairie Chicken (*Tympanuchus pallidicinctus*)

This bird is like a small, pale prairie chicken. It has a restricted range and is perhaps most numerous in Kansas and Oklahoma, for both of these states have hunting seasons for the bird.

It prefers a more arid climate than the greater prairie chicken but is otherwise similar, having even much the same courtship display. [NS]

Blue Grouse (*Dendragapus obscurus*)

Also known as the dusky grouse, the blue grouse is a relatively big bird, averaging 22 inches (56 cm) in length. It occurs in the Rocky Mountains, from Colorado north to British Columbia.

It has salty black upper parts and slate blue underparts. The cock has an orange or yellow comb over the eye; the hens are of a variegated brown color. [NS]

Sage Grouse (*Centrocerus urophasianus*)

This is a large, grayish bird, the cocks of which can be nearly as big as a small turkey (26 to 30 inches/66 to 76 cm), while the hens are smaller. Both cocks and hens have a tail that is long, but not as long as that of the ring-necked pheasant. Their general coloration is brown with a black underbelly; the cocks have a white breast.

The sage grouse inhabits open sagebrush plains in the western United States and eats insects and vegetation, including sagebrush. [NS]

Capercaillie (*Tetrao urogallus*)

The capercaillie, or capercailzie as it is sometimes called in English, is the largest species of European grouse; the cock weighs, on average, between 8 and 12 lb (3.5 and 5.5 kg). It has a wingspan of approximately 50 inches (125 cm) and is some 38 inches (96 cm) long. The hen is much smaller, weighing about half as much as the cock. The capercaillie is a dark bird, ranging from brown to black on its head. Its underside has a dark gray coloration, and its belly is speckled with black and white. There is a bright red spot of naked skin above each eye, and the breast and neck have a dark green metallic look.

It inhabits remote hilly or mountainous areas that are forested, from Scotland and Scandinavia in the north and the Pyrenees in the south, eastward to Mongolia. It lives on a variety of foods, including buds, leaves, pine needles, berries, insects, and grasses.

The mating season starts in late winter and continues until early summer, the exact time being determined more by the weather than by anything else. If warm weather comes early, then the breeding season begins early, too. The mating cock noisily tries to attract the hens in an elaborate ritual that starts about an hour and a half before sunrise.

He begins his song in a favored tree that is used year after year. The song consists of four "verses:" a snapping, a warbling, a sharp popping like the sound of a champagne cork being released, and a hissing. While the bird is hissing, it is deaf to all other sounds, and it can be approached during these few seconds. If undisturbed, the cock repeats his song over and over again until sunrise, when he flies to the ground, and performs a dance for the benefit of the hens he may have attracted.

The bird is known as *Auerhahn* in German. Its name in English derives from the Gaelic *capall coille*, meaning horse of the woods. [TT]

Black Grouse (*Lyrurus tetrix*)

This large grouse is indigenous to most of northern Europe, including southern Scandinavia, and also occurs across Russia and northern Asia to the Pacific Ocean. It is larger than the North American grouse, with cocks being larger than hens: about 2.6 lb (1.2 kg) to 1.8 lb (0.8 kg).

Males are black or bluish-black with a metallic sheen. Their wings are marked with an oblique white bar. The tail feathers are curved in the shape of a lyre, and their underside is white. The hen bird is gray.

Black grouse are found in and at the edges of forests, a type of habitat that intensive farming continues to eliminate. Populations of black grouse have declined recently.

The black grouse, like the capercaillie (see above), has an impressive courtship display: males gobble furiously, beating their wings and extending the head and neck. Nests usually contain eight eggs. [NS]

Hazel Grouse *(Tetrastes bonasia)*

This is a grouse of coniferous woods with a range similar to that of the black grouse. It is about 14 inches (36 cm) long, typically grouse-shaped, but with a longish tail and a slightly crested head. Its head and neck are brownish-red, the underside of its neck is noticeably black bordered with white, its back is a bluish-gray, and its tail is marked with one black and one gray band which show conspicuously in flight. It has a camouflaged appearance and tends to rely on this, rather than on flight, when preyed on by animals and birds. It often perches in trees.

It likes a fairly specific mixture of forest, of which the principal ingredient must be conifer, with admixtures of aspen or alder, birch, and even some juniper; it needs thick undergrowth, too. This habitat occurs over the whole of Europe, with the exception of the British Isles, Denmark, parts of France, and much of the Balkans. Altogether, there are half a dozen subspecies that collectively extend the bird's range right across the Eurasian land-mass to Korea; it is known in Japan, too.

Hazel grouse are monogamous and form pairs without any elaborate ritual in the autumn. When they pair in spring, the cock attracts the hen by emitting a piping sound that can be—and often is—imitated by hunters. [NS]

Ring-necked Pheasant *(Phasianus colchicus)*

This is the pheasant of the Old World. Long-tailed and brilliantly colored, the cock pheasant has a characteristic white ring round its neck, while the hen is smaller, brownish, and has a tail that is longer than that of various grouse, with members of which species it is sometimes confused.

The ring-necked pheasant, which was indigenous to Asia Minor, was introduced into much of Europe by the Romans. There are many species still indigenous to Asia, including China, Mongolia, and Korea. The ring-necked pheasant was introduced into North America in the 1880s, and it is now well-established in many parts of the continent.

It is a bird that prefers to run to cover rather than fly but, when flushed into flight, it utters hoarse croaks and flies strongly, with bursts of wing-beats alternating with glides. It crows when roosting at night.

It is one of several species that have suffered, in North America, from changing farming practices that have reduced the cover it needs, "clean-farming" methods having decimated its population in some areas. Many feel that pen-raised pheasants have diluted the gene pool of once-wild and virile birds. [NS]

Partridge *(European)*

Gray, or Hungarian, Partridge *(North American)*
(Perdix perdix)

Partridge are found from the northern Iberian coast eastward to Russia, through virtually the whole of Europe, including the British Isles, and north to Scandinavia. Three subspecies carry the range across Asia.

Birds from Hungary were introduced into North America, and there are now large populations in Oregon, Idaho, Washington, Montana, and North and South Dakota, smaller but still thriving populations in the Great Lakes states, and still smaller but no less healthy populations in upper New England. In Canada, there are large populations in Alberta, Saskatchewan, Manitoba, and the eastern part of Ontario.

"Gray" partridge is a somewhat misleading name, although the birds have a grey neck and upper breast. They have a pale orange-chestnut colored face and a conspicuous, horseshoe-shaped dark-brown mark on

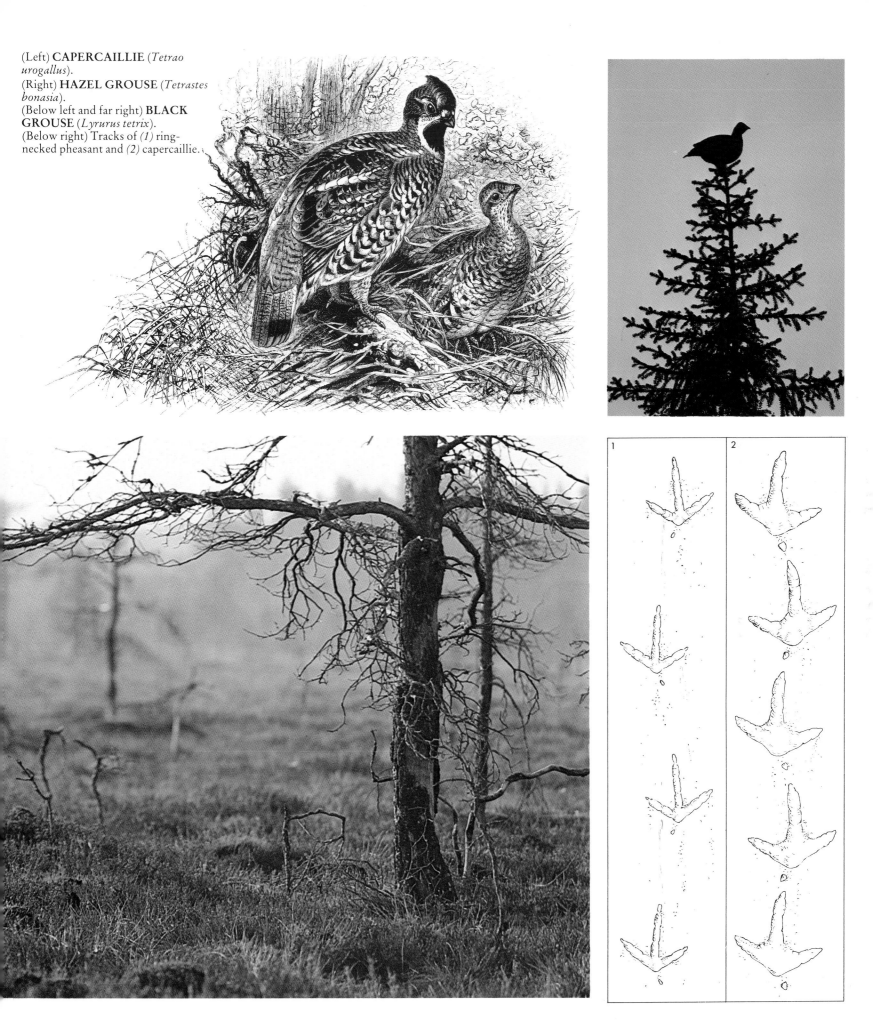

(Left) **CAPERCAILLIE** (*Tetrao urogallus*).
(Right) **HAZEL GROUSE** (*Tetrastes bonasia*).
(Below left and far right) **BLACK GROUSE** (*Lyrurus tetrix*).
(Below right) Tracks of *(1)* ring-necked pheasant and *(2)* capercaillie.

(Above) **RING-NECKED PHEAS-
ANT** (*Phasianus colchicus*). The male
bird.
(Right) **RING-NECKED PHEAS-
ANT** (*Phasianus colchicus*). The
female bird.

(Below upper) **GRAY, or HUNGARIAN, PARTRIDGE** (*Perdix perdix*).
(Below lower) **RED-LEGGED PARTRIDGE** (*Alectoris rufa*).

the lower breast. They are shorter-tailed than the pheasant and much larger than the European quail. The average length is 12 to 14 inches (30 to 36 cm).

Partridge love stubble and grain fields, both for roosting and feeding, and the same parts of fields, plains, or prairies are used year after year. A flushed covey tends to return to the same spot. Coveys normally number up to about twenty birds in late fall or winter, and a covey of this size would include the birds from two nests; this facilitates breeding, for partridge do not breed with siblings. [NS]

Chukar Partridge (*Alectoris graeca* & *A. chukar*)

These species, which have been introduced into the United States, are called rock partridge and chukar, respectively, in Europe; they occur in Italy, Greece, Turkey, and eastward into Asia, on stony and rocky slopes and wooded ground. This corresponds to their habitat in the United States, in the lowland mountains of Idaho, Utah, Nevada, Washington, and Oregon.

Chukars are much smaller than prairie chicken, being only about 13 inches (33 cm) long. The sexes are similar, with an olive-brown back, a white underface patch outlined in black, and buffish flanks marked with eight to thirteen vertical bars of black and chestnut. The chukar gets its name from the sound of its call.

Several species of chukar have a fairly wide range across Asia and are also native to southern Europe. Those in North America are descended from Himalayan and Turkish stock. The European rock partridge utters a ringing whistle rather than clucks and cackles. The chukar requires rather specialized habitat for, while it can withstand cold, it cannot cope with much snow and is therefore most successful in fairly arid or warm regions. In Europe, the chukar is closely related to the red-legged partridge (see below). [NS]

Red-legged Partridge (*Alectoris rufa*)

This bird is native to southwestern Europe, occurring in Portugal, Spain, and southwestern France. It has been introduced to the Azores, Madeira, the Canary Islands, and southern Britain, where it seems to fare best on relatively dry cultivated lands and amid sand dunes. It is slightly larger than the partridge, and the young birds of the two species are very similar.

The adult birds can be identified by a red bill and legs, heavily barred flanks, and a long white stripe above the eye, as against the pale orange-chestnut colored face of the gray partridge, which also has a conspicuous dark-brown horse-shoe mark on its lower breast. The red-legged runs more swiftly. Both species prefer to run than to fly.

When this bird flies, however, it is one of the fastest and, for the shooter, most challenging of the European upland birds. [NS]

Chapter 3
Waterfowl

Canada Goose *(Branta canadensis)*

The most common of all North American geese, with a population well over two million, the Canada Goose is known as the honker, for its habitual call is a loud, resonant honking; this can usually be heard before the birds are in sight when they are migrating. They fly in V-formation.

Canada geese can be easily identified by sight, too, for they have a very conspicuous white patch under their chins, the remainder of their heads and necks being black. Their wings and backs are a dark gray-brown, and their breasts, flanks, and under-tail coverts are white.

Canada geese have been introduced into Europe and New Zealand, but wild flocks appear only in North America. They nest in the northern part of the continent, as far south as the northern United States; most of them winter from the mid-United States to the Gulf of Mexico.

In some regions of North America, they have become troublesome to farmers, for they feed in corn and wheat fields, sometimes in very considerable numbers. [NS]

Snow Goose *(Chen caerulescens)*

This is a white goose with black wing tips. It weighs about 7 lb (3.2 kg) and nests in the extreme north of the American continent and on Greenland, and it winters over much of the eastern United States; some vagrants occur in Europe.

The lesser snow goose (*C. c. caerulescens*) winters mainly along the delta of the Mississippi, on the Gulf coast, in scattered areas of Mexico, and in a few parts of California. The greater snow goose (*C. c. atlantica*) winters along the Atlantic coast, mainly in Delaware, Maryland, Virginia, and southward.

The lesser snow goose can also be of a blue phase—known as the blue goose—when their bodies are a slate-gray; the immature birds are a brownish-gray.

When migrating, the snow goose is noted for long flights and a minimum of stops. These usually occur at staging areas. The geese glean grain fields after the harvest but, in some areas of central Canada, which they traverse before the harvest, they can do considerable damage to the crops. [NS]

Ross' Goose *(Chen rossi)*

Ross' goose is a miniature of the snow goose (see above), being wholly white with black wing tips, a shorter neck, and, in flight, more rapid wing-beats.

It nests in northern Canada (Southampton Island) and winters mainly in the San Joaquin Valley in west-central California, and in some other western states, and in western and central Canada. [NS]

Emperor Goose *(Philacte canagica)*

One of the most beautiful species of geese, adult emperor geese have blue-gray backs edged with black, and then white. Their heads are white, and their bills and legs are pink; immature birds are generally darker.

The emperor goose nests at the extreme east of the Eurasian land mass and in western Alaska, and winters in the Aleutian Islands, on Kodiak Island, and on the Kamchatka peninsula, in Russia. [NS]

(Below) **CANADA GOOSE** (*Branta canadensis*).

Subspecies of the Canada goose. *(1)* Cackling Canada goose (*B. c. minima*). *(2)* Lesser Canada goose (*B. c. parvipes*). *(3)* Vancouver Canada goose (*B. c. fulva*). *(4)* Atlantic Canada goose (*B. c. canadensis*).

(Above left) **BEAN GOOSE** (*Anser fabalis*).
(Left) **BARNACLE GOOSE** (*Branta leucopsis*).
(Above right) **GRAYLAG GOOSE** (*Anser anser*).

White-fronted Goose (Anser albifrons)

This goose can be distinguished by its white facial patch round a pink bill, irregular black and brown markings on its belly, and orange legs; immature birds have yellow legs, and lack the facial patch and the markings on the belly. On the adult birds, the rest of the head and neck, and much of the body, are a grayish-brown. This goose is known to North American and British wildfowlers as the specklebelly.

It has a global distribution, with a breeding range that is circumpolar, except for a few small gaps in the Canadian Northwest Territories, one of which is occupied by the much larger tule goose (*A. a. gambelli*), a subspecies.

White-fronted geese winter on the coasts of North America from southern California, round Mexico, to the Gulf coast and the marshes of Texas and Louisiana, but they are rare on the East coast. In Europe, they winter round the British Isles, the coasts of northwestern Europe from France to Denmark, and eastward in the Mediterranean from Italy. Elsewhere, they are found on the coasts of the Black and Caspian seas, Asia Minor, India, China, parts of Southeast Asia, and Japan. Like other gray geese, they migrate in large flocks, travelling in lines or chevron formation.

It is said that it was geese of this species that alerted the Roman garrison to an incursion of Gauls in 390 BC. [NS]

Magellan Goose (Chloephaga picta)

While not a true goose—the sexes being unalike—but a species of shelduck, the Magellan is the major goose-like bird of South America, with a range extending over the lower part of the continent, and stretching out to include the Falkland Islands. The males are white with black wing tips, and their white back feathers are tipped with black; their feet are black. The females have barred light- and dark-brown breasts and necks, and russet heads; their wings are white below and black above but have white edges at the tips. Their feet are yellow or orange.

They winter in southwestern Argentina but, because they are numerous and grass-eaters, they are unwelcome to the farmers of the region, whose cattle and sheep are thus deprived of food. [NS]

Ashy-headed Goose (Chloephaga poliocephala)

This bird inhabits the same range of South America as the Magellan goose (see above) but is smaller. The two species sometimes fly in formation together but are easily distinguished, for their coloration differs considerably: an ash-gray head and a russet neck and dark chest identify this species, which also has dark, almost black wings with a white leading edge. [NS]

Graylag Goose (Anser anser)

This is a goose of the Eurasian landmass and does not occur in North America. It is one of the largest and strongest of the wild geese. Its coloration is predominately gray, and its head and neck are not darker than the rest of its body. In addition to these characteristics, it can be distinguished from other "gray" geese by its pinkish-gray feet and bill. On long flights, it travels in V-formations, and honks while in flight.

The western (European) race has a thick orange bill. It breeds mostly in Iceland and across the Palaearctic region, and it winters in Britain, the Netherlands, France, Spain, and North Africa.

The eastern race has a thick pink bill and looks lighter, for its feathers have a light edge. It breeds across northern Asia and winters from the eastern Mediterranean to China. An intermediate form is found in western Russia and the Balkans.

Graylags, like many geese, are grass eaters and fly at dawn to their feeding grounds. [RE]

Bean Goose (Anser fabalis)
Pink-footed Goose (A. f. brachyrhynchus)

The bean goose is a Eurasian bird, breeding from Greenland to eastern Siberia and wintering over a large part of Europe and Asia, with a few strays occurring over the Alaskan islands. It is a gray goose and can be distinguished from the graylag, for example, by its yellow feet and its black and yellow bill (those of the graylag are, respectively, pinkish-gray and orange or pink). It is a rather large goose.

In fall and winter, it feeds heavily in grain-stubble fields, favoring barley, but it also eats a wide variety of other vegetable food.

The pink-footed goose is another gray goose, but slightly smaller than the bean. It has a very dark head, a small pink beak, a relatively light toned body, and pink legs. It has a more restricted range than the bean goose, breeding in Greenland, Iceland, and Spitzbergen, and wintering mostly in the British Isles, northern France, Belgium, Holland, and Germany. Pink-footed geese occasionally appear in other parts of Europe, including Russia. They rest in the Faeroes and Shetlands en route to Scandinavia. They fly in skeins of over 1,000 birds, with family groups of adults and goslings keeping together, a habit common to a number of species of geese. Pink-footed geese gather in large flocks on moors, sandbanks, marshes, estuaries and other coastal lands. Except when hungry, as on arrival from migration, they are difficult to approach, being very wary. [RE]

Barnacle Goose (Branta leucopsis)

Smaller than the Canada goose, and white-faced while the Canada goose is white only under the chin, the barnacle goose is predominately a European bird; it occasionally appears on the Atlantic coast of North America. It is markedly a black-and-white bird, with the black of its neck extending down to its breast, and with black feet and bill; its upper parts are a lavender gray. Its call is a short, shrill, repeated bark.

It winters mainly in Denmark, on the German coast, in the Netherlands, and in Ireland and Scotland. It nests in the high Arctic.

While it is known as the "little nun" in France, on account of its coloration, it was once believed, according to a Welsh writer in 1187, to grow on trees and, in Ireland, to be a sort of fish, being eaten as such on fast days. [NS]

Brant, or Brent, Goose (Branta bernicla)

This is a small dark goose, hardly bigger than a mallard drake. There are three distinct races that differ from one another in their range and degree of darkness of plumage. Brant geese of all species have black heads, necks, and chests, and brilliant white rear-parts. Their total range encompasses the entire Arctic, while they migrate southward in winter and appear in northern Europe and Asia, and in North America.

The dark-bellied, or Russian, brant (B. b. bernicla) has a dark gray-brown belly; it nests to the north of Europe and Asia, and migrates along the coastlines in winter. The light-bellied, or Atlantic, brant has much paler under-parts that contrast strongly with the relatively darker upper-parts; it breeds in eastern Canada, Greenland, Spitzbergen, and the Franz Josef archipelago, and migrates southward in winter along the Atlantic shores. The dark- and light-bellied brants can occur in the same flocks, or gaggles. The third subspecies is the black, or Pacific, brant (B. b. nigricans or B. b. orientalis). It is much darker than the other two. It breeds on the islands and coasts of Siberia, Alaska, and western Canada, and winters on the Pacific coast from southwestern British Columbia to Baja California.

Brants are more maritime in their habits than most geese, resting on the water, and feeding in shallow coastal waters, often up-ending to do so. On short foraging flights, they often fly in low, ragged flocks and on longer flights form wavering lines, but not regular formations. [RE]

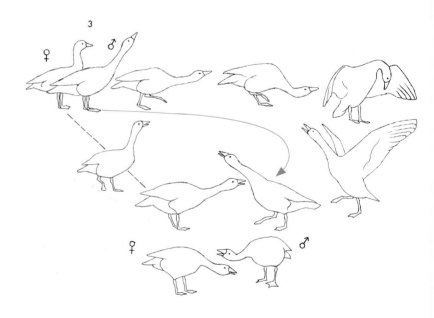

A Communication among geese is well-developed. *(1)* When a goose prepares to fly, it signals to others of the same species in the flock. *(2)* A graylag goose shakes its head from side to side so that its red beak is noticeable; a Canada goose raises its head so as to display the conspicuous white patch on its cheeks and neck. *(3)* An intruding goose is seen off: a gander advances with its head extended and held successively lower. The intruder, head drooping and with wings spread as if protectively, turns away. The triumphant male "goose-steps," flaps its wings, and stretches out its neck exultingly. As he rejoins the female, she trusts her head forward toward him, but lower than his. (Right) **BRANT, or BRENT, GOOSE** (Branta bernicla).

(Above and opposite, top left) **SHOVELER** (*Anas clypeata*). (Below) **MALLARD** (*Anas platyrhynchos*). (Opposite, top right) **COMMON, or NORTHERN, SHELDUCK** (*Tadorna tadorna*).

(Opposite, center) Surface-feeding ducks, such as the mallard *(1)*, have their legs placed centrally under the body; the legs of diving ducks *(2)* are to the rear. Surface-feeding ducks fly up from the water with a spring *(3)*, while diving ducks patter along the surface for some distance before becoming airborne *(4)*.

Other Geese

There are a number of species of geese in various parts of the world, of which one—the Hawaiian nene goose—is recovering from a condition of near-extinction. Other species include the swan-goose, the bar-headed goose, and the red-breasted goose of Asia; the Cape Barren goose of Australia; an African sheldgoose known as the Egyptian goose, which is actually a sort of long-legged duck; and three sheldgeese of South America—the ruddy-headed goose, the Orinoco goose, which is a forest dweller, and the maritime kelp goose. [RE]

Shelducks *(Tadornini)*

Shelducks have short, narrow, goose-like bills, and most species have white upper and under wing coverts and iridescent green specula, and their downy plumage is strongly patterned.

Probably the most abundant and widespread is the common, or northern, shelduck (*Tadorna tadorna*), which breeds from the coast of western Europe eastward through much of Asia. This species is slightly larger than a mallard. The sexes are colored alike, but the male is larger and has a large frontal knob on his bill; at a distance, the birds appear black and white. Their heads and necks are a dark, metallic green, bills are bright red, and bodies mostly white but with a broad brown band across the breast. The legs are orange. The tip of the tail, the wing tips, and a broad band along the rear edges of the wings are black.

The ruddy shelduck (*T. ferruginea*) has a breeding range that covers small parts of southern Europe, northernmost Africa, and much of Central Asia. It migrates deep into Africa and down the southern coasts of Asia, but unlike the common shelduck, it is an inland bird. Almost uniformly rusty or orange-brown in coloration, its head is pale, its bill and legs are black, and its wings and tail are marked with black; there is

white on its wing coverts. The male has a small black neck-ring.

Other species of shelduck include the Cape shelduck of South Africa, the New Zealand shelduck, the Australian shelduck, and the radjah shelduck, which is an Australian species, but occurs also in the East Indies. [RE]

Mallard *(Anas platyrhynchos)*

This is the common bird of the entire northern hemisphere—the brightly colored drake with his cocky, curled rump feathers, and the brown, comparatively drab duck. They breed over virtually all their range, and they migrate as far south as North Africa, Southeast Asia, and southern Mexico. There are Hawaiian and Laysan Island races, too.

Mallard have adapted to human settlement about as well as pigeons and are thoroughly at home in cities and urban parks—fat, comfortable, nearly domesticated birds that occasionally breed with domestic strains.

Nevertheless, truly wild mallard are wary and shy of man, particularly hunting man. [NS]

Shoveler *(Anas clypeata)*

The common, or northern, shoveler is found throughout North America, Europe, and Asia, and it occasionally visits South America, Africa, and even Australia.

While it is a small duck, a little smaller than a mallard, it can be identified, even in flight, by its disproportionately large, spatulate bill, which is widest near its rounded tip. When migrating, both sexes are brownish, the male being in molt and thus hardly brighter than the female; they can then be mistaken for teal or, later, for small mallards. The male is otherwise colorful, with a green head, like that of a mallard, a

Pintail (*Anas acuta*) in flight. Their slender, pointed bodies are a distinguishing mark even at a distance. Of the pair to the left, the male bird has a predominantly white body and a dark head and rear part.

white breast, reddish-brown flanks and belly, a black rump with a sooty tail with whitish outers, and a slaty brown back. Both sexes have orange feet, a blue wing patch, and green specula.

Shovelers are found in fresh, brackish, and salty shallows. In some North American regions—notably California, Louisiana, and northern Mexico—there are large wintering populations; some birds fly to Hawaii from breeding grounds in Alaska. They breed over much of Europe, but not in Italy or Spain. [RE]

Gadwall *(Anas strepera)*

Gadwall of both sexes are sometimes taken for female mallard, although the male gadwall is predominantly grey but with a black rump, while the female has a yellowish-orange bill with dark markings (the female mallard's is orange); both sexes show a white patch on the wing in flight, whereas the female mallard has white-bordered blue specula. Mallards have less pointed wings.

While found all over the world except in South America and Australasia, gadwall are nowhere very abundant. They migrate early in fall, like some species of teal, and their passage is usually over by the end of October. [NS]

Pintail *(Anas acuta)*

Pintail are second only to mallard in numbers, and the northern species of pintail breeds round the entire arctic region, from Iceland through Scandinavia, the northern parts of Russia to Siberia, and through Alaska and much of Canada to Greenland. Pintail migrate southward into large parts of Africa, lower Asia, and South America; some winter on Pacific islands. An antarctic species is found on the islands in the south of the Indian Ocean; other species are native to the West Indies, to South America, and Africa.

The male of the northern pintail is characterized by white sides and a white front to its neck, a brown head, and a long pointed tail. The female is brownish, with a less markedly pointed tail, and otherwise looks rather like a female mallard, but without the wing specula. Pintail are about the same size as mallard, but slimmer, and with longer necks. In flight, while the mallard male's white neck ring is noticeable, the pintail male has a white streak running up toward its head from its under-parts.

Pintail fly extremely fast and tend to fly higher than most ducks, even when approaching a resting or feeding place. On short flights, they fly in small ragged groups, in twos or threes, or singly. On longer flights, they fly in large skeins, sometimes breaking into rippling arcs or ellipses.

Their wings are raked and pointed, and their bodies streamlined. They are far more wary than mallards. [NS]

Black Duck *(Anas rubripes)*

This duck is not really black, but dark brown, stippled with buff or creamy white on the feather edges; in winter plumage, adult males have a U-shaped line, adult females a V-shaped line, on the small feathers on the sides of the chest. In the air, black ducks appear, to experienced observers, like dark, very large female mallards, but with long sooty, flat-bellied profiles, large heads, a moderate wing-beat, and wide, only moderately curving wings.

Their major breeding grounds extend across eastern Canada but stretch to include part of the eastern United States and, to the west, the prairie provinces of Canada and the adjacent parts of the United States. The birds that breed in the west of this range migrate south along the Mississippi valley, but the rest, the majority, winter from New England down through the coastal states to North Carolina; the greatest concentration occurs on the Delmarva Peninsula at the junction of Delaware, Maryland, and Virginia.

The black duck is diminishing in number, for it is shyer and less adaptable than a mallard, for example, and cannot adjust to human disturbance of its environment. [NS]

Duck species are far too numerous for all to be given space here or even named; those that are mentioned are the most commonly hunted over the widest areas. Other duck of hunting interest include the torrent duck of the Andes; the blue, or mountain, duck of New Zealand; the falcated duck of eastern Asia; the mallard-like yellow-billed duck of Africa; the Australasian spot-billed duck; the Philippine duck, another mallard-like species; several shoveler or shoveler-like species occurring in South America, Africa, and Asia; the harlequin, the oldsquaw or long-tailed, and the goldeneye or whistler duck—all of them widely distributed sea ducks, but often found on inland waters; and the bufflehead. There are, too, localized races of the mallard, known by various names in the areas where they occur. [RE]

Wood Duck *(Aix sponsa)*

Smaller than the mallard, the male wood duck is, perhaps, the most strikingly colored of all North American waterfowl; it can also be identified by its head-crest, which slopes down from the back of its head. The female is without brilliant markings but has a darkish, crested head

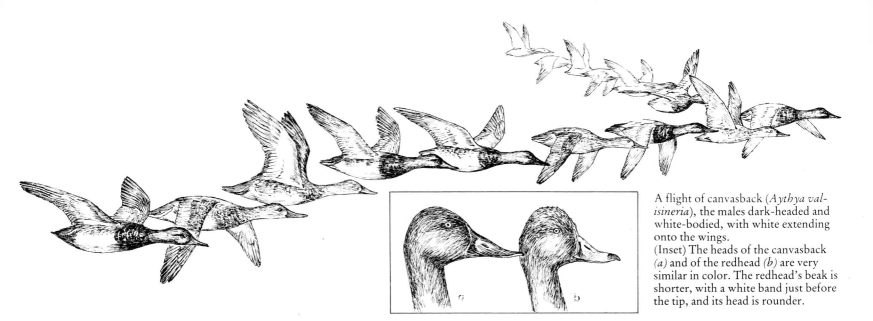

A flight of canvasback (*Aythya val-isineria*), the males dark-headed and white-bodied, with white extending onto the wings.
(Inset) The heads of the canvasback (*a*) and of the redhead (*b*) are very similar in color. The redhead's beak is shorter, with a white band just before the tip, and its head is rounder.

with a conspicuous white patch round the eye. It is brownish, with light flanks contrasting with darker wings. In the air, wood duck show a contrast between a white belly and darker wings and breast; their square tails are noticeable, too. On land, they have a markedly upright stance, like all tree ducks.

They inhabit wooded, swampy country over most of the eastern United States northward to Canada and, in the west, from central California to southern British Columbia. A major wintering area is the valley of the Mississippi southward of Illinois to the coastal marshes of the Gulf of Mexico; others are the marshes and tidal rivers of the Atlantic and Pacific coasts.

Wood duck nested, until comparatively recently, only in hollow trees, but human destruction and management of woodlands have made these scarce. The ducks have adapted, however, to the specially designed nesting boxes provided by conservationists, game managers, and others, and wood duck populations, which at one time had fallen to dangerously low levels, have made a remarkable comeback.

A number of other species, similar in some respects to the wood duck, are occasionally hunted in widely separated parts of the world. Among the more significant of these are the mandarin duck of east Asia, the males of which are even more highly colored than the male wood duck; the Australian wood duck, or maned goose, of which the males are more dully colored than the females; the Brazilian teal, a small South American percher; the ringed teal of the southeastern part of South America; the wild form of the muscovy duck, with a range from Mexico to southern Brazil; and the white-winged wood duck of southeast Asia. [NS]

Fulvous Tree-duck (*Dendrocygna bicolor*)

This is a brownish, long-necked, almost goose-like duck, of which the sexes are alike. Its long legs are noticeable, both when it is on the ground and in the air, when they trail beyond the tail. A white stripe along its side separates the darker wings from the lighter flanks. In the Americas, it is common from Mexico to northern Argentina, and extends north-ward only to the southwestern United States. It occurs also throughout most of eastern Africa, on Madagascar, in India, and in some other parts of Asia.

In its Central and South American range, it occurs together with another tree-duck, the red-billed, or black-bellied, which is less common than the fulvous. Both species are also known as whistling ducks, the fulvous having a squealing, whistling call that can perhaps be rendered as "chee-weee."

There are six other species of tree-duck and, like the two mentioned here, they fly with slow wing beats, but they are so trusting that they circle round hunters, for whom they represent very poor sport. One of them, the lesser whistling duck of India and southern Asia (*D. javanica*), is additionally not only small and drab in appearance, but unpalatable too, having a downright unpleasant taste. [NS]

Canvasback (*Aythya valisineria*)

Slightly smaller than a mallard, the canvasback male is a white-bodied duck with head patterning like that of the pochard and redhead (see below), but with a distinctive long bill that gives its head a sloping profile. The female shares this profile but has a grayish hue, although with about the same patterning.

Canvasback breed in the prairie provinces of Canada, in the Yukon, in Alaska, and in a few parts of the upper United States. They winter in considerable numbers in the area of Chesapeake Bay on the East coast, in San Francisco Bay in slightly less substantial numbers, and also along the coasts of the gulfs of California and Mexico.

At one time, canvasback were extremely plentiful, but they declined significantly under the impact of market shooting, drought, and the draining of wetlands, and have never really recovered. Their favorite food, the wild celery, grows in fresh or brackish, but not salt, water, and it, too, has declined. To make matters worse, the closely related redhead duck (see below) sometimes lays its eggs in canvasback nests, thereby reducing the chances of survival for the eggs and ducklings of both species. [RE]

Redhead (*Aythya americana*)

A North American pochard, this bird is similar in appearance to the European pochard, except that the female has an indistinct face patch and is uniformly brownish (the female of the European pochard shows a contrast between a darker head and a lighter body). The ring-necked duck (*A. collaris*), a slightly smaller bird, can be confused with the redhead but has (in the male) a black head and back and (in the female) a dark back and darker head; ring-necked ducks have shorter bills than redheads.

Redhead breed primarily on the potholed prairies of central Canada and the Bear Lake region of northern Utah. They migrate along all the major American flyways, some reaching central Mexico, but with large numbers staying on Chesapeake Bay and the sounds inside the Outer Banks of North Carolina. Sometimes, eighty percent of the redhead population winters along the Gulf coast, from Florida to Yucatan.

Like the canvasback, the redhead has suffered from the effects of industrial activity on wetlands, and its total numbers have declined. [RE]

European, or Common, Pochard (*Aythya ferina*)

Pochards are diving ducks that are fast in the air, flying with a quick wing-beat, but they are poor walkers. One of the more common species is the European pochard, which ranges from Britain across Europe and through much of Asia.

It is about the size of a mallard. Both sexes have grayish wings and dark-gray feet; the male's head is dark reddish-brown, the female's is brown or grayish-brown. The male's breast is black, the female's colored like her head. Their bodies are, respectively, grayish and brownish.

Pochard breed in freshwater regions, but during migration and in winter, some species, including this one, are also to be found in brackish estuaries, tending to gather in large flocks.

Pochard are wary and difficult to approach. Like all diving ducks, they run over the water to gather speed for flight, for their wings are short. [RE]

Greater Scaup (*Aythya marila*)

A bit smaller than the mallard, the male of the greater scaup (the North American name) has black fore-parts, a black head with a greenish sheen, a dark rump and tail, and a light gray back; its under-parts are white. Virtually the only difference between it and the male of the ring-necked duck is that the latter has no white stripe showing through the wing primaries. The males of greater and lesser scaup are virtually impossible to distinguish apart in the air, for they are almost the same size, but the male of the lesser scaup has a purplish head, and a crown that is more pronounced and is almost a tuft.

The female greater scaup is a brownish duck with a clear white patch round the base of its bill; this and the white wing stripe are the only features by which it can easily be distinguished from the female of lesser scaup, ring-necked duck, and redhead.

Greater scaup have a nearly circumpolar breeding range, perhaps the most famous nesting grounds being those on the tundra ponds and potholes of Alaska; there are other nesting grounds in Canada, northern Europe, and Asia. Some of the birds remain surprisingly far north in winter, but other migrate along the sea coasts of Europe, Asia, and North America; they prefer maritime wintering habitats, where they sometimes gather in enormous flocks, feeding near shore in the early morning or near dusk. They are inquisitive and may approach a strange moving object that is not recognizably human. [RE]

Lesser Scaup (*Aythya affinis*)

This is a North American species. It is essentially a pochard of the interior of the continent, for it winters more over inland waters than the greater scaup (see above). It looks almost exactly like the greater scaup, and the differences between the two species, such as they are, are noted above.

Lesser scaup nest from Alaska through central Canada, and in some of the upper central and western United States. They migrate southward as far as Panama, but some remain relatively far north.

Lesser scaup eat more vegetation than do greater scaup; another difference is that the lesser is a decidedly more wary and suspicious bird than the greater. [RE]

The species of *Aythyinae* named above are the most commonly hunted diving ducks, the group which includes goldeneyes and pochards. Other in the group are the southern pochard of South America and Africa; the rosy-billed pochard of lower South America; the red-crested pochard,

(Above) **GOLDENEYE** (*Bucephala clangula*).
(Opposite, top) The goldeneye's typical mating display.
(Opposite, center) **PINTAIL** (*Anas acuta*).
(Opposite, bottom) **BLUE-WINGED TEAL** (*Anas discors*).
(Right) Duck species in flight may be distinguished by the coloration of their wings and specula. *(1)* Cinnamon teal; *(2)* blue-winged teal; *(3)* green-winged teal; *(4)* common teal; *(5)* mallard; and *(6)* black duck.

with a range from southern and eastern Europe through Central Asia; the Australasian white-eye; the ferruginous white-eye of southern Eurasia; the Baer's pochard of eastern Siberia; the New Zealand scaup; and the Eurasian tufted duck, which resembles the ring-necked duck mentioned above. [RE]

Sea Ducks

Sea ducks include mergansers, eiders, and scoters. In general, merganser are less maritime than other sea ducks but still rely heavily on fish and other aquatic animals for food, and share some other characteristics with sea ducks.

Merganser have long, narrow, almost cylindrical, sawtoothed bills, in contrast to the heavy bills typical of other sea ducks. Some merganser are crested, some are quite colorful. The common merganser (*Mergus merganser*) of Eurasia and North America is known to many European hunters as the goosander.

Eider (*Somateria mollissima*) are larger, more arctic, and far more maritime ducks. The females are brownish, the drakes generally patterned in black and white, though the heads of some species are colorful. Most species have black wings with white covert patches; some have colorful bills. Typical of eiders is a leathery bill extension, or shield, which runs up onto the forehead. They tend to fly low, usually in a line. The scooter is closely related to the eider. The drakes are black or nearly so, the females are a dark, grayish brown. The white-winged scoter (*Melanitta fusca*) has a white speculum and is the most widely distributed scoter, being found in North America, especially across Canada, and along the coast of Europe from Portugal to Scandinavia. [RE]

Common Teal (*Anas crecca*)

Called simply teal in Britain, this bird is a little more than half the length of a mallard; it is the smallest European duck, and one of the smallest in North America, where it can occur on the East coast.

Both sexes have a green and black speculum pattern and gray feet. The female looks like a very small mallard female—a mottled brown bird with a pale or white belly. The drake has a black bill and a chestnut head with a broad, curving, green eye stripe with a narrow light or white outline that is faint or absent in the American green-winged teal (see below), which also lacks the common teal's horizontal black and white stripe above the wing. The green-winged teal, however, has a vertical white stripe between flank and breast—the common teal lacks this.

Both species sometimes occur together on the Atlantic coast of North America. The common teal breeds in Iceland and over much of Europe and Asia; it migrates far to the south, reaching as far as a line between the Gulf of Guinea in the west to the Gulf of Aden in the east in Africa, and reaching as far south as Sri Lanka and Malaya in Asia. [NS]

Green-winged Teal (*Anas carolinensis*)

A very small duck, about half the size of the mallard, the green-winged teal breeds in Alaska, Canada, and the upper United States, the most productive nesting area lying between the Mississippi River and the Pacific coast. It migrates as far south as Central America, though the greatest wintering concentrations are in upper Mexico and along the Gulf coast of the United States.

Green-winged teal are hardy birds which, in some parts of their range, are among the very late migrants, but they seldom linger at waystops where they rest and feed.

The green-winged is hard to distinguish from the common teal (see above, where both are described). In flight, both appear dark-headed, small, and white-bellied. They feed in the water, up-ending to reach bottom growth, and sometimes feed on land. A characteristic call by the male is a whistling. [NS]

Blue-winged Teal (*Anas discors*)

The blue-winged teal is a purely American species. It is slightly larger than the green-winged or common teals (see above), and both sexes have brownish wings with green specula and a large, unmistakable light-blue patch formed by the upper coverts; in bright sunlight, this patch can appear white. The male has a bluish-gray head with a conspicuous, white facial crescent in front of, and extending back over, the eye. In dim light, it is hard to distinguish this teal from either the green-winged or the cinnamon teal (see below).

Blue-winged teal nest in the greatest numbers in the area between the Great Lakes and the Pacific. They migrate as far south as Chile and Argentina, with a major concentration gathering in Columbia on the marshes at the mouth of the Magdalena River, which lies to the northeast of Panama. Other concentrations are found in Florida, the coastal marshes of Louisiana and Texas, and, in Mexico, in Culican and the Yucatan Peninsula. They also winter on Cuba and in Guyana.

Blue-winged teal feed on flooded rice fields, freshwater marshes, ponds, sloughs, and creeks; they eat mostly vegetation. They fly low, fast, and erratically, often in tight clusters. [NS]

Cinnamon Teal (*Anas cyanoptera*)

Like the blue-winged teal, the cinnamon teal is an American species. The two species are about the same size, have about the same behavior, and occupy the same habitat.

The cinnamon teal has the same blue wing patch as the blue-winged teal, but the male is a rich cinnamon brown, with a black rump, while the female is slightly more rusty in color, and has a longer, wider bill. While all ducks occasionally dive to escape danger, the cinnamon teal is among the most adept at swimming long distances underwater.

Major breeding grounds are in the states of Washington, Idaho, and Utah, and the largest wintering concentration gathers in Mexico. Several subspecies occur in South America. [NS]

Baikal Teal (*Anas formosa*)

This species breeds mainly in Siberia, migrating and wintering throughout much of eastern Asia, with a few accidentals straggling into Alaska. Major wintering grounds include southern Siberia, eastern China, Japan, Mongolia, and Korea.

The female has brown and buff plumage and looks rather like a female green-winged teal (see above), except that she has a conspicuous pale buff cheek mark. The male is one of the most handsome of ducks, having a unique head pattern of buff-yellow, green, and black, with each of these colors trimmed with white. The sides and breast are spotted, and the wings are brown with green specula.

In behavior and habitat, this teal resembles the more common varieties described above. [NS]

South American Green-winged, or Speckled, Teal (*Anas flavirostris*)

Both sexes of this teal are pale-brownish and speckled with darker brown heads (there are teal from the northern Andes, however, with quite gray heads). The speculum is like that of the common teal (see above); the bill is sometimes yellow and sometimes as dark as that of the green-winged teal of North America.

The South American species occurs in various parts of western and southern South America, and its habitats and behavior are roughly like those of the other teal described above. [NS]

Several other varieties of teal with limited distribution are hunted in different parts of the world. They include the silver teal (South America), the tiny Hottentot teal (Africa and Madagascar), the Cape teal (southern and central Africa), the gray teal (East Indies, Australia, and New Zealand), and the teal sometimes considered a reddish variant of the gray, the Madagascar teal. There is also the chestnut teal of Australia and Tasmania, the brown teal of New Zealand and the adjacent islands, and the marbled teal, sometimes held to be of another genus, which ranges from the Mediterranean to southwestern Asia. Finally, there is the Eurasian garganey. [RE]

Baldpate, or American Widgeon *(Anas americana)*

This is a common medium-sized dabbling duck, slightly smaller than a mallard. The male is brown and has a whitish forehead and crown, a marking often visible when the birds are in flight, or as they rise from fields or water; the female has a grayish head and a brownish body.

Baldpates nest throughout southern Canada and, in smaller numbers, in Alaska and a few states south of the Canadian border. The greatest concentrations are in Canada's central prairie-pothole region. Large wintering concentrations gather in central California, the Mississippi Delta, and on parts of the coast of the Gulf of Mexico.

Baldpates frequent freshwater ponds and marshes, and brackish and salt marshes and bays. Although they feed on crops and in gardens, they are primarily aquatic feeders; being poor divers, they feed in company with other species that dive, canvasbacks and scaup, for example, so as to feed on the vegetation that floats to the surface as these other ducks feed underwater. [NS]

European Widgeon *(Anas penelope)*

The male of the European widgeon is most readily distinguished from that of the American widgeon or baldpate (see above) by a buff, rather than a white, forehead and crown, and a bright orange-brown or chestnut face and neck, in contrast to the baldpate's green eye stripe. The females are similarly brownish, but the European widgeon is tawnier on the head, and a more dusky brown on the body. Both sexes of the European widgeon have white upper wing coverts and green specula patterns, those of the female being a dingy white or gray, with less green.

European widgeon breed on Iceland, in Scotland, in the upper parts of Scandinavia, and eastward through northern Russia. They winter over large parts of Europe and Asia; birds from Europe visit the Atlantic coast of North America with a frequency that is debated by ornithologists and wildfowlers there, and birds from the eastern end of their breeding range, in Asia, visit the Pacific coast of North America. These visits occur mostly during the fall or winter, while the interior of North America has been visited by European widgeon in spring.

European widgeon have behavior and habitats very close to those of the baldpate. [NS]

In addition to the two widgeon of the northern hemisphere described above, there is a widgeon of South America, the Chiloé *(Anas sibilatrix)*, from the south of the continent. It is the only dabbling species of which the female has a brightly colored head. Both males and females have iridescent green heads, their flanks are orange-brown, and their breasts have a scaly-looking black and white pattern.

One sometimes hears of a bird called a "Cape widgeon," but this is, in fact, a misnomer for the Cape teal *(Anas capensis)*, which is bigger than other teal. Both sexes of the species have pink bills, green and black specula broadly bordered with white, and are otherwise mottled gray. [RE]

Male ducks are commonly but not invariably more brightly colored or more clearly marked than the females. *(1)* European widgeon; *(2)* American widgeon; *(3)* Australian teal *(Anas gibberifrons gracilis)*; and *(4)* Baikal teal.

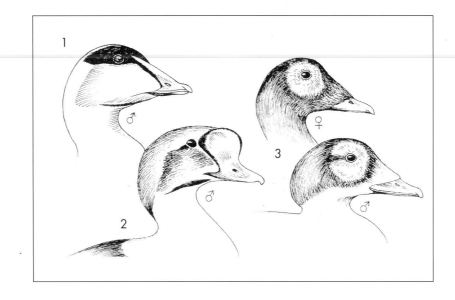

(Above) Other eider include (1) American eider
(S. m. dresseri), (2) King eider (S. spectabilis),
(3) the female and male spectacled, or Fischer's,
eider (S.fischeri).

(Below) European eider, female on the left,
male on the right.

III The History of Hunting

Chapter 1

The First Recreational Hunters

John F. Reiger

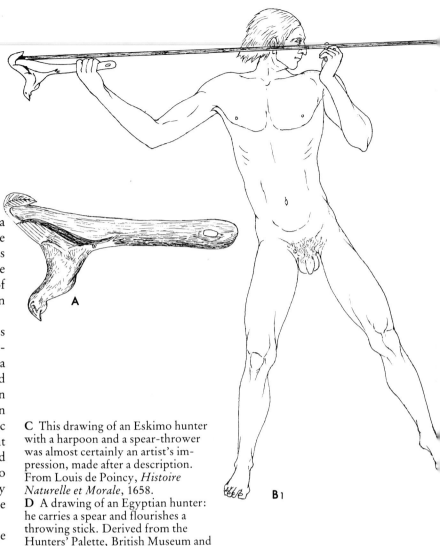

Throughout almost all of man's evolution as a species, he has been a hunter. Only yesterday, after more than a million years, did he emerge as a "modern" being: urban, industrialized, and cut off from his natural habitat and the creatures he used to hunt. "The exciting life of the Stone Age hunter still survives in our social dreams, as an expression of our biological past," writes René Dubos, the eminent French-born American biologist.

After many decades of a seeming bias of scholars against the qualities of the primitive hunting and gathering peoples—savages who had preceded the "advanced" farmer—a new interpretation has been offered by a growing number of anthropologists and prehistorians. Indeed, one could almost say that the earlier interpretation of man's development has been turned on its head. Now some scholars suggest that man's undoing began when he became a farmer, and that he not only lost much in a psychic and spiritual sense, but that it was then that his war on the environment began in earnest. As a hunter, he had learned to be alert, self-reliant, and ingenious in outwitting the craftiest game. He had also learned how to cooperate in group activity and how to share the kill. Virtually every physical and mental development that supported the survival of the "naked ape" derived from the hunting life.

In prehistory, the change from a hunting–gathering economy to tillage and domestication of beasts is the beginning of settlement and "civilization." According to the traditional scenario of historical events, man now had a predictable food supply, and therefore he could devote more time to leisure and creativity. He now developed cultures with social stratification, complex religions, large-scale building projects and, finally, the written word or symbol that marks the transition from prehistory to history.

There are, of course, many exceptions to this tidy format. At least two North American Indian peoples, for example, developed social stratification and a rich artistic life, but exceptions notwithstanding, man became settled and "civilized" after he took on the role of the farmer, and not before. Some recent scholars argue that civilization had its price. Man now saw the creatures sanctified by hunting ritual as predators on his crops. Indeed, every living thing that failed to fit into the microcosm which agricultural man had designed for himself was, if possible, ruthlessly eliminated.

The farmer became a prisoner of the weather and the land that had once nurtured his spirit as well as his body. Instead of being able to wander with the tribal group, the individual and the group were now tied to a tiny parcel of land, the constant worry being that natural forces could, in a single stroke, wipe out an entire year's work. In short, agriculture may have marked the rise of what is generally accepted as civilization, but it also signaled the beginning of man's enslavement to given place.

However uncomfortable the life of the Stone Age hunter, his days were filled with *meaningful* activity. His hunting was part subsistence

C This drawing of an Eskimo hunter with a harpoon and a spear-thrower was almost certainly an artist's impression, made after a description. From Louis de Poincy, *Histoire Naturelle et Morale*, 1658.
D A drawing of an Egyptian hunter: he carries a spear and flourishes a throwing stick. Derived from the Hunters' Palette, British Museum and Louvre.

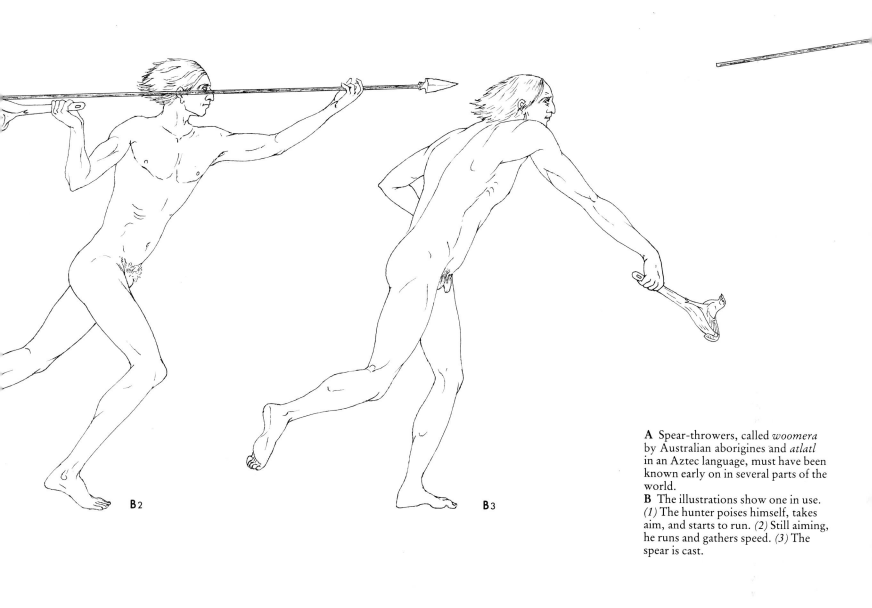

A Spear-throwers, called *woomera* by Australian aborigines and *atlatl* in an Aztec language, must have been known early on in several parts of the world.
B The illustrations show one in use. *(1)* The hunter poises himself, takes aim, and starts to run. *(2)* Still aiming, he runs and gathers speed. *(3)* The spear is cast.

and part religion, part work and part pleasure. Historians of hunting generally draw a sharp distinction between the chase as recreation and the subsistence hunting of prehistoric or primitive societies. Although there are obvious reasons for the distinction, it may be more revealing to base a history of hunting on the thesis that, even for Stone Age man, the subsistence hunt was also a form of recreation—an activity that elicited pleasure apart from providing food.

That his hunting could have been *more* than a chore required for survival is suggested by the magical feeling which radiates from the paintings in the famous caves at Lascaux and Font-de-Gaume in France and Altamira in Spain. I first saw the masterpieces of Font-de-Gaume in the summer of 1964. Their aesthetic effect and the response they aroused in me, a modern recreational hunter, may be inferred from my diary entry for 25 August of that year:

"The entrance to the cave is on a hillside, and looks exactly like every painting or drawing I have ever seen that has endeavored to reproduce what life must have been like in that prehistoric period. . . . Most of the paintings, or I should really call them sketches, were of bison, horses, great stags . . . smaller deer, and mammoths. . . . The paintings were mostly done by Cro-Magnon people and were of two major periods; one group was from about 17,000 years ago, the other from over 25,000 years ago. Evidently, the cave was used by one band of people for a time,

deserted, and later discovered by another, totally different group, who added their artistic endeavors to another section of the cave.

"The artists were clever in that they incorporated the contours of the cave walls into the painting itself in order to give the subject more of a feeling of movement and life—this attempt at realistic depiction is clearly preconceived and not the least bit accidental.

"It was appreciation and affinity that I felt for these primitive human beings and their evidently unquenchable desire to recreate their environment. Imagine two or three of those element beings crouched next to that same cave wall 20,000 years ago, with one or more holding a torch, while the respected artist traced his wet, stained finger over the surface and created something very much like the bison the family group killed the day before. Perhaps, when the artist was finished, the entire group came nearer, holding their torches ever closer to the masterpiece, and they all grunted with satisfaction and, undoubtedly, joy."

Despite their antiquity, these Cro-Magnon peoples were among the first of our own species, *Homo sapiens* ("wise man"). Their wisdom developed out of surviving the challenges of a demanding environment; they had already displaced the first real hunter, the Neanderthal man, and refined the latter's hunting tools and methods.

Perhaps the earliest hunting implement was a club, one of the large bones of a prey animal killed by disease, accident, or predators. At some

A A moose spear is shown here from the side. When the moose moved against a line (*a*), a catch (*b*) was released. The spear (*c*), which was mounted on a young tree-trunk under tension, was then flung forward.
B Moose impeded by deep snow could fall to the spears of hunters on primitive skis.

point, a man-like creature must have wielded a large bone as a club and realized how useful it could be when facing beasts which had such formidable weapons as bone-like horns, hooves, and teeth. Utilized (as distinct from made) bone clubs were possibly the first hunting weapons.

The only other real contender for this honor would have been a heavy stone, simply picked up and thrown at an animal or bird. Even the giant cave bears of Europe were killed or disabled by boulders cast down on them from fairly high elevations by the later Neanderthal hunters.

Here, the tendency to imitate nature would probably have come into play. After seeing the results of an avalanche that trapped and killed animals, the earliest man-like beings may have endeavored to duplicate, in a small way, the deadliness of a hurtling projectile.

At this point, one might ask if the early hunters pursued the bigger mammals instead of the smaller, less dangerous, species, and if so, why? Hunting bands probably found it easier (and relatively more rewarding) to trap large, slow-moving beasts, such as mammoths, rather than the smaller, quicker animals. This is particularly true of large animals like the bison, which can be driven into snow and rendered almost helpless. Interestingly, this technique of catching and killing game "mired down" in snow was a hunting technique used in North America and Europe as late as the early years of the twentieth century.

Another likely reason for pursuing large game animals in the Pleistocene epoch, but one overlooked often, was the need for one-piece furs to cover an individual's body. In the intense cold of the Ice Ages and before man learned to sew, the largest mammals with the thickest coats may well have been even more important for clothing than for food.

Once again, the development of man's reason and spirit of cooperation made up for his vulnerability. The same two traits would also allow him to fashion hunting weapons and methods that would eventually make him the most formidable animal of the Pleistocene.

The cave bear had once been an important quarry of Stone Age hunters, but when climatic changes transformed the ecosystems of Central Europe, the mammoth became the major source of food there and, according to recent archeological work, in North America as well. The ancestors of the American Indians crossed the Bering Strait (a land bridge when glaciation had drastically lowered the water level) between Siberia and Alaska in a series of migrations that took place about 25,000 years ago.

Both in Europe and North America, the mammoth was probably pursued into deep snow or muddy swamps, where it mired down and could be killed. One scholar suggests that they might also have been taken in huge "deadfalls," a sort of trap that would have killed or disabled an animal after it sprang the "trigger." On entering the deadfall and springing the trap, the mammoth was apparently knocked down by heavy logs. The scholar does not suggest how such heavy logs could be lifted so high, however. Another probable trapping technique was the use of pitfalls, deep holes dug in the ground and thinly covered with branches and leaves as camouflage.

Enough social organization would have been achieved by this time for us to hypothesize the technique of using beaters to drive the animal toward the trap or pit, or to the place where it would mire down. Archeological excavations have revealed that, in some regions, the hunters worked together to drive large game animals over cliffs. Even when trapped in a deadfall or pit, the beast would usually have to be killed by spears or other tipped weapons.

The horse became extinct in North America before the appearance of the first human, but it was to succeed the mammoth in Central Europe as the major prey species of the Stone Age. Wild horses traveled in great herds, and their gregariousness and speed proved to be their undoing. Initially, fires were set to drive the animals in the general direction of a cliff, and beaters and obstructions were placed along the sides to keep the animals running in the desired direction toward the precipice. The

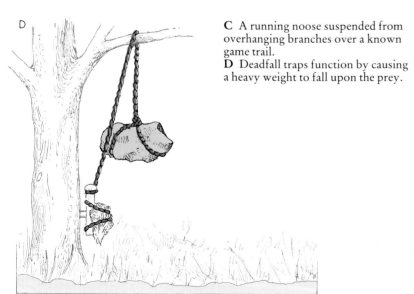

C A running noose suspended from overhanging branches over a known game trail.
D Deadfall traps function by causing a heavy weight to fall upon the prey.

momentum of the animals behind pushed the ones in front over the edge.

At Solutré, near Lyons, is a famous horse-hunting site with the remains of over 10,000 horses at the base of a precipice. One estimate puts the total number of horses killed there at over 100,000. Used for centuries, the site reached the peak of its usage about 40,000 years ago.

Just as the cave bear had been replaced by the mammoth, and the mammoth by the horse, now the horse was to be replaced by the reindeer as the major prey species of the later Stone Age hunters of Central Europe. Although the animal had been occasionally hunted as far back as Neanderthal times, it was only with the last great period of glaciation that the reindeer would become the primary game animal.

Reindeer grazed in huge herds as the horses had, and the Stone Age people pursued them with the same techniques as those they had found so useful in bringing down horses. They used fire and beaters to drive the reindeer, but not over precipices, for the most common method seems to have been to drive the animals into rivers, where they became all but helpless. North American Indians used similar methods in hunting deer, and even as recently as the late nineteenth century, Indian hunters in New York State used hounds to drive whitetail deer into lakes where they were killed from canoes.

By the time the reindeer became the chief quarry of the late Stone Age people, European hunters were using weapons that made them most accomplished predators. Chief among these were the bow and arrow and the spear-thrower, or *atlatl*. The latter weapon is a short stick with a notch or cup at one end in which the spear end is placed. The atlatl, of course, is not thrown with the spear but is retained in the hand. The device gives the thrower added leverage by acting as an extension of the hunter's arm and has been shown to add as much as sixty percent to the distance attained by a hand-thrown spear. Recorded in Europe, North America, and Australia, it was used also by the Eskimo, as it is useful when hunting in a boat, because one hand can be used to steady the craft.

Along with the advances in weaponry in the late Stone Age came the beginnings of agriculture and animal domestication. The latter may have begun when the young of quarry that had been killed were caught and preserved. Dogs must first have appeared as scavengers about the hunters' encampments and, although they were eaten until prehistoric times, they were among the first animals to be utilized as hunting allies.

While hunting and food-gathering were the exclusive sources of food in the early Stone Age, they must have become less important later. Kitchen middens of the later Stone Age from sites in Europe warrant this conclusion, for only a relatively small proportion of the bones identified by archeologists are of wild species, all the rest being of domesticated animals.

With the "Great Change" of the beginnings of settled agriculture, man would begin to try to transform the natural world rather than endeavor to live off it. His life would become less unpredictable and his chances of survival less uncertain. For these reasons, no doubt, he was willing to settle for the drudgery and boredom of a largely agricultural existence.

Hunting bands would become small settlements, of which the population grew with the food supply. The settled tribes defended their agricultural and grazing lands against other tribes. But people must still have been able to move on to other territory for, during thousands of years, the overall population density remained extremely low. The richest and most easily used farming and grazing lands were limited, existing only in certain types of ecosystems, and competition for these favored localities must have been great.

Before the change, the strongest and most athletic members of the group were the most active hunters. After it, they became warriors when necessary, either providing protection for the rest of the tribe or harrying its neighbors. The strongest of these warriors became chiefs, and the seeds of a stratified social society were sown.

Chiefs and perhaps their descendants came to be accorded, or to acquire, certain privileges, none more inviolate than that of hunting wild animals. Larger areas of land were tilled, and larger herds of domesticated animals were grazed. Hunting lands gradually shrank and came eventually to be monopolized and protected so the game on them could survive. This development must have taken several thousand years. Hunting, once a necessity for survival, and as such permeated with sympathetic magic and religion in the minds of Stone Age hunters, had become a symbol of social status, being, for the first time in history, *purely* a recreation—a sport.

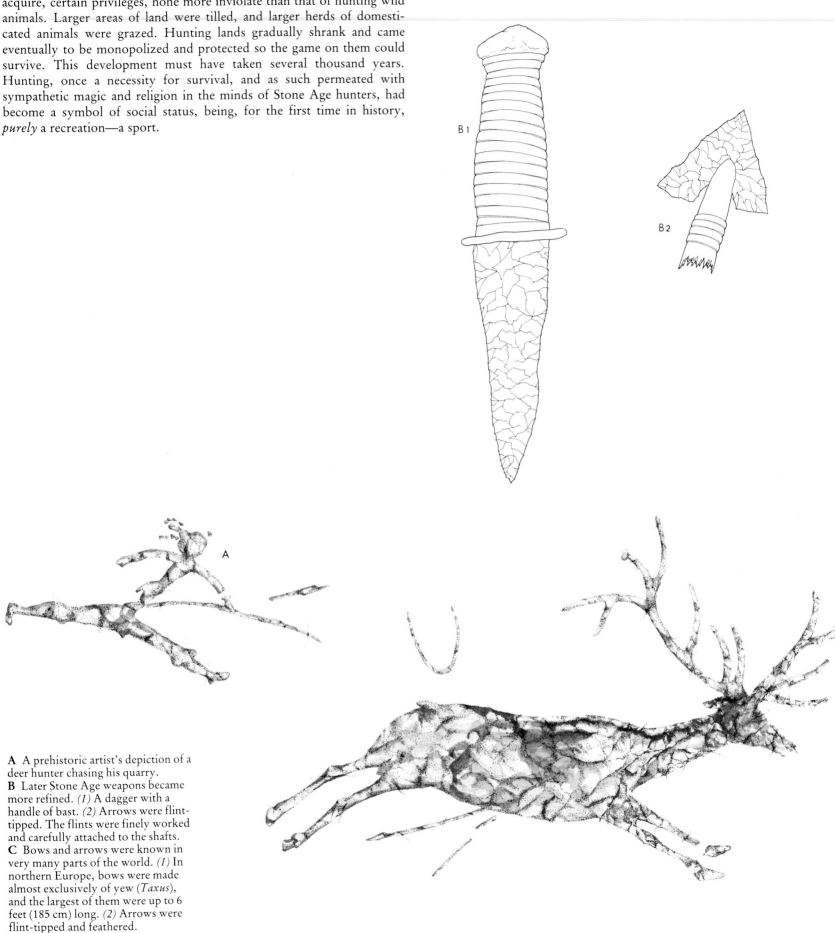

A A prehistoric artist's depiction of a deer hunter chasing his quarry.
B Later Stone Age weapons became more refined. *(1)* A dagger with a handle of bast. *(2)* Arrows were flint-tipped. The flints were finely worked and carefully attached to the shafts.
C Bows and arrows were known in very many parts of the world. *(1)* In northern Europe, bows were made almost exclusively of yew (*Taxus*), and the largest of them were up to 6 feet (185 cm) long. *(2)* Arrows were flint-tipped and feathered.

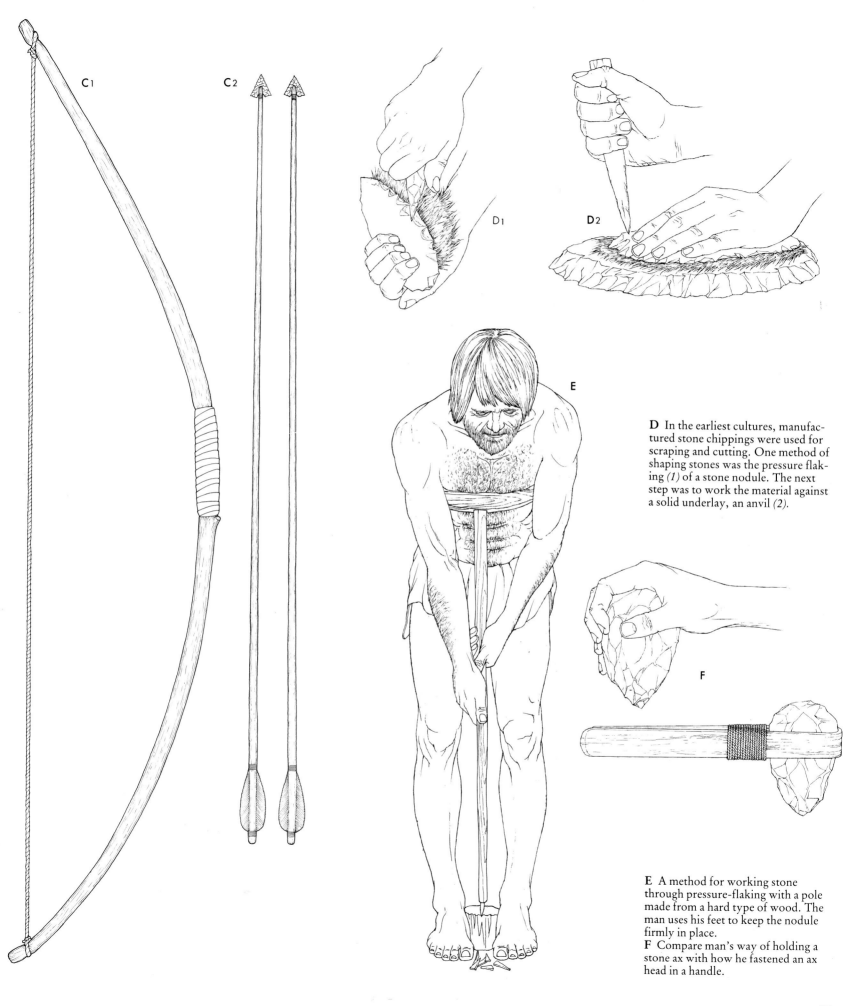

C₁

C₂

D₁

D₂

E

D In the earliest cultures, manufactured stone chippings were used for scraping and cutting. One method of shaping stones was the pressure flaking *(1)* of a stone nodule. The next step was to work the material against a solid underlay, an anvil *(2)*.

F

E A method for working stone through pressure-flaking with a pole made from a hard type of wood. The man uses his feet to keep the nodule firmly in place.
F Compare man's way of holding a stone ax with how he fastened an ax head in a handle.

Chapter 2

Hunting from Early Times to the Middle Ages

John F. Reiger

Many non-hunters might say that, when hunting became unnecessary for survival, it became a "mere" recreation and thus decadent, but they would fail to understand that there is nothing more important in life than recreation. According to *Webster's New International Dictionary*, "to recreate" is "to cheer ... renew or enliven ... refresh after wearying toil or anxiety ... give fresh life to." Hunters have always been fortunate in that their favorite recreation is as significant for them as their vocations. For many, it is more significant.

For these hunters, it has not been enough to live comfortably. One must live with vitality and dedication. In his *Meditations on Hunting* (1942), the Spanish philosopher José Ortega y Gasset wrote: "Other living beings simply live. Man, on the other hand, is not given the option of simply living; he can and must dedicate himself to living. ... And it happens that many men of our time have dedicated themselves to the sport of hunting. Furthermore, throughout universal history, from Sumeria and Acadia, Assyria and the First Empire of Egypt, up until the present now unraveling, there have always been men, many men ... who dedicated themselves to hunting out of pleasure, will, or affection."

The symbolic importance of hunting to the rulers of the great ancient civilizations is obvious if one scans art-history volumes. It is little short of amazing how many of the illustrations depict hunting scenes. Just a few examples are the wild-oxen hunt on the Egyptian temple of Rameses III (1195–1164 B.C.) at Thebes and the famous fowling scene from another Theban tomb; the Assyrian king hunting lions, from the palace of Assurbanipal (669–626 B.C.) at Nineveh, and the magnificent "Dying Lioness" at Nineveh, showing a lioness pierced with arrows, rearing up for a last attack; and, finally, the Persian king Chosroes I (531–570 A.D.) hunting ibex from horseback—the creation of a silversmith in the sixth century A.D.

Though from different periods and places, what all of these art works have in common is vigor and visual reality. As one art historian observed, "natural forms have been recorded with the same keenness of observation we noted in prehistoric cave paintings."

After studying the hunting art of the great ancient civilizations, one is compelled to agree with Ortega y Gasset that the hunter is, perhaps more than others, the "alert man," for "only the hunter, imitating the perpetual alertness of the wild animal, sees everything."

From the historian's point of view, the pictures of hunting are, perhaps, most important for their depiction of what was hunted and how.

Although the ancient Egyptian peasantry hunted for food, the pharaohs and their courts hunted for pleasure, sometimes employing coursing dogs that looked like the modern greyhound. A scene from King Tutankhamun's bow case shows one of these dogs running alongside a gazelle-like animal, while seizing one of the animal's front legs in his jaws. The young pharaoh rides behind in his chariot, about to loose an arrow at the animal his dog is slowing down for him.

Hunting from a chariot pulled by two speedy horses seems to have

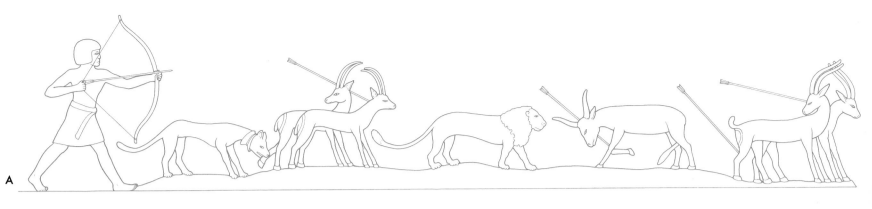

A

A Part of a painted relief from Ti's tomb in Sakkara, Fifth Dynasty, 2563-2423 B.C. In addition to the long-tailed hunting dogs shown here, the relief depicts some short-tailed hunting dogs of about the same size, and one much smaller dog, seemingly herding a bull. Among other animals shown is a rabbit and what looks like a pair of hedgehogs.

B Reality or a hunter's dream? Tutankhamun and dog despatching five lions and two lionesses. The pharaoh, who may be drawing his bow left-handed, has three full quivers in reserve, after loosing off fifteen arrows. From a painted wooden chest in the tomb of Tutankhamun at Thebes.

B

been the preferred method of pursuing big game. The bow and arrow was widely used for less dangerous prey, while the spear was more often reserved for formidable beasts such as lions and wild oxen.

Small game was also widely hunted by the Egyptian rulers. Among the most famous examples of all Egyptian tomb art is the wildfowl-hunting scene from Thebes already mentioned. The hunter stands in his boat as it moves deep into a swamp filled with very tall papyrus, and he apparently knocks down pintails and other ducks as they are flushed ahead of the craft. The weapon used is a long, S-shaped throwing-stick. In one hand he holds three fluttering ducks by the feet. It is not certain whether they are game, just taken, for they may be live decoys used to attract passing flocks.

One thing is certain, however. Given the abundance of waterfowl then on the Nile and the flocks of ducks that must have risen in front of the hunter's boat, his heavy throwing-stick was an effective weapon when hurled into their midst. As strange as it may seem to us, it appears that the waterfowler's *cat*, and not a dog, retrieved the downed birds.

The ancient Assyrians, too, hunted big game from chariots, but they seem to have preferred the bow and arrow, even for the fiercest animals. One famous scene shows an enraged lion, already pierced with several arrows, climbing into the back of the king's chariot, while, at point-blank range, he shoots an arrow at it.

That the Assyrians liked their hunting dangerous is shown by another work of art. At Nineveh, it depicts the king hunting lions on horseback. This time he is using a spear, which he is thrusting down a lion's throat while the beast stands on its hind legs, apparently ready to pull the king out of the saddle. Behind the hunter, a second horse is being attacked on its flanks by a lion with three arrows in it, probably shot earlier by the king.

Both the Assyrians and the ancient Persians loved hunting so much that they built huge walled enclosures where game was kept until the king and his party were ready to pursue it. In a single hunt, one Assyrian ruler claimed to have killed 450 lions, 390 wild oxen, 200 ostriches, and 30 elephants, while capturing scores of other animals that would be put into the enclosure and pursued another time. It should be noted that the word "paradise" comes from the ancient Persian and refers to a hunting park or enclosure.

With the rise of classical Greece and Rome, hunting was followed as eagerly as before, the main difference being that we know far more about it as a result of greater surviving documentation. Both pictorial art and classical literature convey the popularity of hunting for sport, at least among the upper classes.

But hunting was more than popular; increasingly, it came to be seen as an all-important part of the training for manhood, both physically and symbolically.

In Plato's *Republic*, Socrates, Plato's former teacher, says to a fellow philosopher: "Now then, Glaucon, we must post ourselves like a ring of huntsmen around the thicket, with very alert minds, so that justice does not escape us . . . Look out then and do your best to get a glimpse of it before me and drive it toward me."

Plato ends his hunting metaphor by having Socrates exclaim: "By the devil! I think we have a track, and I don't think it will escape us now."

Clearly, Plato is telling the reader that the philosopher, seeking justice, should aspire to the same habits of mind that the good hunter possesses.

While Plato and other philosophers and their students were familiar with hunting, the Greek soldier-historian, Xenophon, lauded it for its physical and military influences. In his *Cynegeticus*, the first known handbook on hunting, he states: "Men who love sports [hunting] will reap therefrom no small advantage, for they will gain bodily health, better sight, better hearing, and a later old age. Above all, it is an excellent training for war."

The way the chase was practiced at this time seems to indicate that Xenophon was correct in his high estimation of its physical benefits to the hunter. While the bow and arrow may still have been used in utilitarian hunting, the spear seems to have been the most commonly employed sporting weapon. Spears were of two types: light javelins for throwing and heavy spears for jabbing at close range. One can believe that hunting encouraged mental and physical alertness in those who, armed only with a spear, struggled with an enraged wild boar!

(Hunting boar with only a spear, or with a spear and a short game sword, was an honored custom in Europe for hundreds of years; and as late as the twentieth century, several daring sportsmen both in Europe and North America briefly revived the tradition. Though the practice is far too dangerous to be recommended, the bravery inherent in it commands admiration.)

Boar were invariably hunted with dogs, the idea being to drive them into nets where they became entangled and could be dispatched with spears. Xenophon tells us, however, that the plan sometimes failed, and hunters then found themselves alone, at least for a time, with free-ranging boars.

Perhaps the most significant fact about the chase in this period is that it was a sport and not degenerate butchery. Boar hunters, for example, were on foot, armed only with spears. Their main objective seems to have been to work the dogs, some of which were almost as large as wolves, and to outwit the boar by maneuvering it into the net.

While the weapons of European hunters would change radically in the future, the *essence* of the hunt remained the same: there would be no true sport unless the animals had a fair chance of escaping, unless dogs participated in the chase, and unless there was at least some risk to one's person, however theoretical that risk might be. As the eminent Swedish historian of hunting, Gunnar Brusewitz, states, "it is certainly no exaggeration to say that the European sport of hunting has its roots in Rome and Greece."

According to Brusewitz, hare hunting in ancient Greece is an excellent example of "the show's the thing"—that the chase, rather than the kill, is what makes the hunt. For example, Xenophon recommends that, when a hare is being pursued by hounds, it should be allowed to get away "for the glory of the goddess of hunting." Two thousand years later, the French scientist-philosopher Pascal put it another way: "The virtue of the hare is not in having it but in the pursuit of it."

It should also be mentioned that hare hunting along the Danube, the northern border of the Roman Empire, exemplifies the still-current notion that only the "better class" can fully appreciate the hunt, for the rich rode after the hounds on horseback, while the poor followed on foot. The English sport of fox hunting, later brought to the American colonies, emphasizes the glories of the chase, while playing down the kill; it certainly has the same concern for social distinctions.

Along with some other components of classical Greek culture, the Romans retained Greek ideas concerning the hunt. Xenophon was especially influential. But with the spread of decadence in the Empire, hunting, too, began to suffer.

Even those who have not visited the Colosseum, built between 72 and 80 A.D. and capable then of holding 50,000 spectators, have heard seemingly lurid tales of gladiators fighting lions and slave girls being torn apart by starved crocodiles. What is remarkable is how many of these stories are uncomfortably close to the truth. Animals were brought to the Colosseum and other arenas from the corners of the Empire, and whole provinces were depleted of the larger mammal forms. Hunting had degenerated into bloodletting.

It was the fall of the Western Roman Empire in 476, some tidy-minded historians argue, that signaled the beginning of the Middle Ages in Europe. Whatever the exact date for its inception, the period continued through the Reformation and the Renaissance until the Age of Discovery. Of all the forms of hunting widely practiced in medieval times, the one that left an indelible mark is falconry, which had been practiced in Asia long before the Middle Ages began in Europe. Known for centuries on the steppes of Turkistan, an area today divided by the Russian-Chinese frontier, the sport spread east and west with the movements of conquerors and migrating peoples. After knowledge of the sport was introduced, its popularity increased apace as long as two requirements were met: a steady supply of falcons and open country in which to enjoy the aerial spectacle.

Once again, we have an excellent example of the belief that sport, and not bloodletting, is what is important. In falconry, the hawk sometimes released its prey unharmed after forcing it to the ground.

A common prey in Europe were herons. The falconer would fly his hawk at the large, slow-moving herons while they flew between their fishing areas and their rookeries.

Falconry was once open to all, but it soon came to be a pastime reserved only for the upper ranks of society. An emperor alone was entitled to fly a golden eagle or a kite, while medieval English law specified that a king was entitled to a white Greenland falcon, naturally considered the next best, a duke to a peregrine, and a knight to a goshawk. The falcon became a badge of rank, and themes relating to falconry permeated art and literature.

Printed in 1486, the first book on hunting in England is the "Boke of St. Albans," which thoroughly discusses falconry. A persistent, but seemingly groundless, legend connects the book with a Dame Julians Barnes, who is said to have been born in 1388. The book, however, reveals that the clergy—notwithstanding their official condemnation of falconry—were as much interested in the sport as were the laity outside the church.

Despite the fame of European falconry, we should not forget that the East was where the sport was born, and at the same time that Europeans were enjoying their "aerial ballets," the great Kublai Khan was enjoying his—and on a somewhat larger scale. When Marco Polo visited the Chinese ruler in the thirteenth century, he reported that the Khan went hunting with "10,000 falconers and some 500 gyrfalcons, besides peregrines . . . and other hawks in great numbers, and goshawks able to fly at the water-fowl . . . ."

The devotion of European nobility to the ancient sport of falconry failed to prevent its decline, which was hastened as more and more land came under the plow, and as shooting, and game preservation, became more widespread. Along with the Industrial Revolution and the spread of towns, these trends hampered the falconer and his bird, because they no longer had the unrestricted use they had once enjoyed of the still-remaining great expanses of open, park-like country.

Like falconry, other forms of hunting in the Middle Ages were seen by the aristocracy as their special prerogatives. King Dagobert, a Frankish ruler, was the first to establish regulations for hunting game in Europe. Under his seventh-century "forest laws," only the king and his nobles had the right to hunt. Later, in 1016, King Canute enacted the first game law in England, which prescribed the penalty of death for anyone hunting in the king's forests.

"Under Canute," according to hunting historian Michael Brander, "the old Saxon way of hunting with hayes, or hedges laid in funnel shape, through which the game was driven to the waiting hunters, was still the principal method used." The object was to kill the beasts with arrows or spears as they ran past.

After the Norman conquest in 1066, hunting methods radically changed, as did much else in England. Now, instead of driving the game to waiting hunters, the usual technique was to hunt the prey on horseback, with dogs.

A bloodhound was employed to track a stag to its bed. Once the animal was alerted, other hounds were brought up and released, with the horsemen galloping behind as best they could. Horns were sounded to keep the hunters in touch with each other until the dogs brought the stag to bay.

It is not difficult to see the close evolutionary relationship between this kind of hunting and later British and North American fox hunting. In fact, the patrons of this sport on both sides of the Atlantic often use the term "hunting" to mean this form of the chase, and no other. Even a dilettante in the sport has heard of the hunting cry of "Tally-ho!", which is a corruption of the Norman cry of "*Thialau!*".

How to hunt the hippopotamus: the harpoons have detachable heads to which are attached ropes. A strike in the animal's nostrils enables the hunter to keep the hippopotamus from submerging, but how could the hunters keep their light craft from overturning? From Sakkara, Fifth Dynasty.

B A falconer's equipment includes *(1)* a heavy gauntlet, worn to protect the hand and wrist from the claws and beak of the bird as it perches on, or returns to, the fist. A small piece of meat, firmly held between finger and thumb, encourages the bird to return. When it does not, a bell *(2)*, attached by a soft leather strap, called a bewit, to the bird's leg, is a useful means of locating the bird. *(3)* This hood, elegantly feathered, is in the Dutch style. It must be made so as to cover the bird's eyes without in any way damaging them.

A A peregrine falcon *(1)* waiting for quarry and *(2)* at the end of her stoop, where she has killed a cock pheasant. On the ground, a falconer has just sent off a falcon. A further four birds, all hooded to prevent them from seeing quarry too soon, perch on the frame—a cadge—borne by the cadger. In the background, a mounted falconer is having trouble keeping his bird on his wrist.

The falconer wears a heavy gauntlet, usually on the left hand. The bird perches on it and is prevented from flying away by the jesses, which the falconer holds in his left hand. With the bird so held, the falconer must be dextrous in manipulating the hood and in leashing and unleashing the bird.

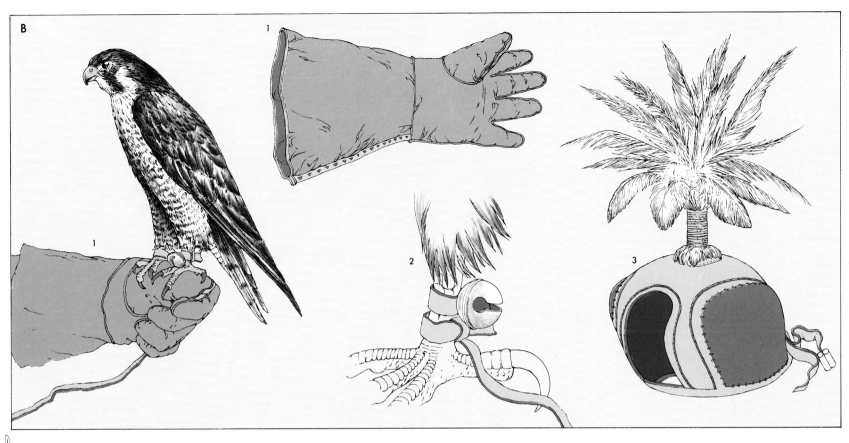

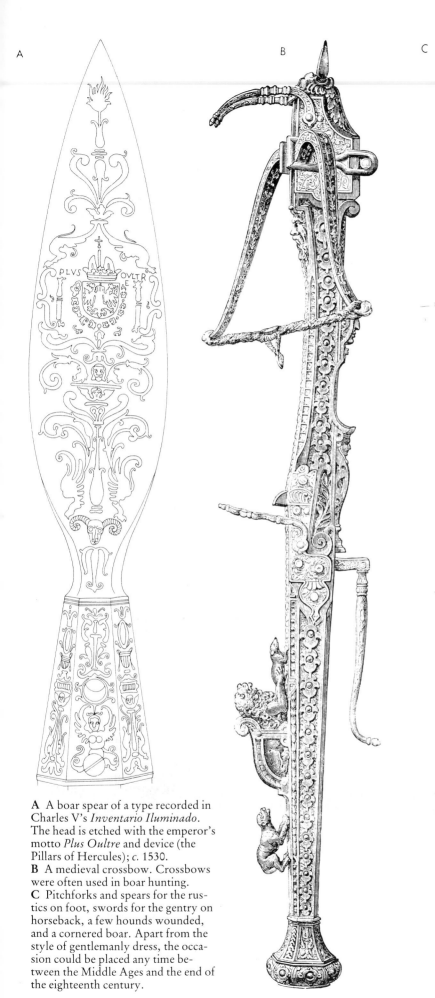

A A boar spear of a type recorded in Charles V's *Inventario Iluminado*. The head is etched with the emperor's motto *Plus Oultre* and device (the Pillars of Hercules); *c.* 1530.
B A medieval crossbow. Crossbows were often used in boar hunting.
C Pitchforks and spears for the rustics on foot, swords for the gentry on horseback, a few hounds wounded, and a cornered boar. Apart from the style of gentlemanly dress, the occasion could be placed any time between the Middle Ages and the end of the eighteenth century.

95

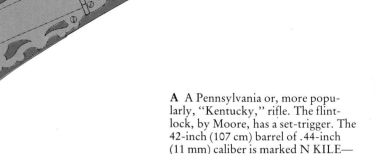

Chapter 3
The Age of Firearms

John F. Reiger

While the Norman conquest of England produced great changes in that country, a far larger change was in the making as the ships of Christopher Columbus left the Spanish coast behind them. More than any other event, Columbus's first voyage in 1492 signaled the end of the Middle Ages. Indeed, the single most important theme in world history from the beginning of the sixteenth century to the beginning of the twentieth was the movement of European peoples and cultures into every corner of the globe.

At the time of the early explorations, eastern North America was not a howling wilderness, as many still believe. Rather, it was a land already modified by the agricultural and hunting practices of an Indian population far greater than was believed even a few years ago. Most of the Eastern Woodland Indians had economies based partly on agriculture and partly on hunting-gathering traditions.

Trees were girdled and then burned off to create open spaces for the growing of crops of corn and beans, and fire was used to drive deer and other game ahead to waiting hunters. The resulting open areas in the woods, which later developed into second-growth forest, were responsible for the great abundance of species like whitetail deer, ruffed grouse, and turkey, which the Europeans found on penetrating the wilds. If the woods had been unmodified first-growth forests, with a thick canopy of branches overhead and little or no ground cover, the specific wildlife the Europeans encountered would have been nonexistent or in far smaller supply. The three species cited above all require variety in their habitats, particularly "edges" where woods and fields come together.

Many of the basic hunting techniques used by the Indians were precisely those employed by the Stone Age ancestors of the European invaders. And while Indians sometimes hunted for sport, they specialized in trapping many animals at one time, the object being to obtain as much meat as possible. Deer were driven into stockade-like enclosures or into water or deep snow, where they became virtually helpless. As already noted, fire was often employed to move the game in the desired direction.

Though the European settlers and explorers seldom used the Indians' techniques of mass slaughter, they did adopt some of their methods when pursuing individual animals. In central Europe during the Middle Ages (and as late as the Renaissance), hounds had sometimes been used to drive stags into ponds or rivers where mounted lancers speared the game. In eastern North America, this method was revived in a modified form based on the Indian practice of using dogs to drive deer into lakes, where they were killed from canoes. This cruel "sport" was not halted until the late nineteenth century.

Another type of hunting learned from the Indians was "jacklighting," sometimes called "firelighting," a nighttime endeavor. One man held a torch behind the hunter as the two men moved slowly through the woods. Stunned by the illumination, the game would freeze in its tracks, and the hunter aimed at the light reflected by the animal's eyes.

While this technique was most commonly employed in deer hunting, it

A A Pennsylvania or, more popularly, "Kentucky," rifle. The flintlock, by Moore, has a set-trigger. The 42-inch (107 cm) barrel of .44-inch (11 mm) caliber is marked N KILE—1817.
B Handgunners shooting at birds. From Tartaglia, *Three bookes of Colloquies . . .*

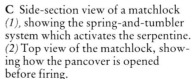

C Side-section view of a matchlock *(1)*, showing the spring-and-tumbler system which activates the serpentine. *(2)* Top view of the matchlock, showing how the pancover is opened before firing.
D A seemingly ingenious means of stalking. Early eighteenth century.
E A beautifully engraved French wheel-lock, 1665.

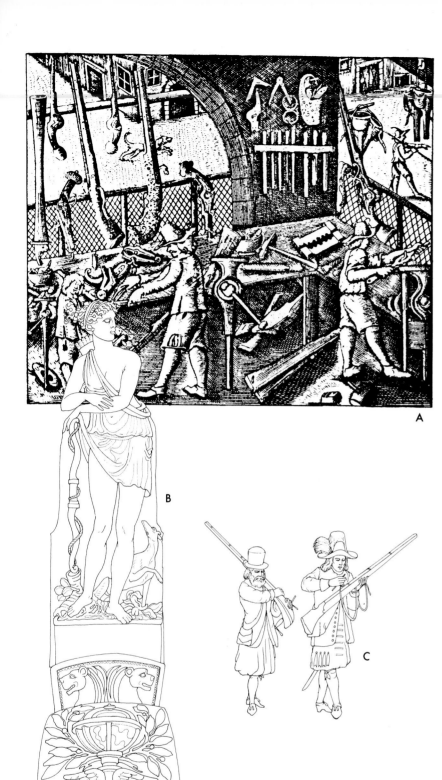

also proved to be deadly to waterfowl. Commercial hunters, in particular, frequently mounted a light in the bow of a skiff and, with muffled oars, rowed slowly down on rafts of ducks and geese. On dark, calm nights, the birds would hardly move until the gunner behind the light was at point-blank range.

This form of unsportsmanlike hunting is by no means dead. With the coming of automobiles in the twentieth century, the ancient method has been revived by poachers, who blind deer with their headlights. This activity is still all too common in many parts of America.

It may seem strange to some that the Europeans should adopt Indian hunting techniques, when the Indians had "primitive" weapons and the whites firearms. Though gunpowder was probably known in ninth-century China and came into use in Europe in the fourteenth century, the development of guns suitable for hunting was not particularly rapid. The first portable guns, made around the middle of the fourteenth century, were dangerous to handle and required a support when fired. Although the early "hand cannon" was unwieldy and inaccurate, it was sufficiently useful in warfare to prompt further experimentation with improvements in mechanism and design. Some of the soldiers who accompanied Columbus were armed with an early, rather crude form of matchlock harquebus, but this, too, was better suited to warfare than to hunting, and the Columbus expedition carried additional small arms, including crossbows.

One of the earliest designs for a wheel-lock firearm was drawn by Leonardo da Vinci. Wheel-lock guns, which were an enormous improvement, began to appear at about the beginning of the sixteenth century. They provided faster, surer ignition than the matchlock, of which the match could sputter and die, and they were easier to aim.

Wheel-locks were sometimes used in Europe for hunting. They were gradually replaced by snaphaunces, miquelets, doglocks, and other early versions of the flintlock, and firearms came into wider and wider sporting use. One must bear in mind, however, that flintlocks were cumbersome, heavy, and unreliable by modern standards.

The eighteenth century had nearly ended before the great English gunsmiths—particularly Henry Nock—succeeded in improving the ignition system sufficiently to achieve a full, efficient burning of the powder charge in a relatively short barrel. In 1786, Nock perfected a breech that transmitted the flash from the priming pan to the charge in the barrel much more rapidly. It was chiefly this improvement that brought about a transition in smoothbores from long, heavy fowling pieces to light, graceful shotguns and thus led to the acceptance of the double-barreled gun that was to become classic.

Among rifles, one early type was far superior to the rest. This was the *Jäger* rifle—the "huntsman's rifle"—chiefly a German design wedded to the excellent French flintlock and destined to become popular throughout much of continental Europe. It was used for early target competitions, and in warfare as well as for hunting. A full-stocked, relatively short-barreled rifle, it was characterized by a rather large bore and extremely fine crafting of the lock, sights, rifling, and stock contours. Typically, it had a box with a sliding lid recessed into the buttstock for carrying small tools, flints, and greased patches.

This box was to survive into the percussion period—usually as a compartment with a hinged lid—for carrying percussion caps and patches. The *Jäger* was the direct antecedent of many fine European and English hunting rifles. It was also an important forerunner of the sporting carbine. It came to the New World in the eighteenth century with German and Swiss emigrants, and there it was gradually transformed into a lighter, much slimmer, longer-barreled, smaller-bored, graceful firearm that was at first known as the American rifle.

The *Jäger* had been designed specifically for hunting deer, boar, and chamois. The American rifle was more versatile. Because of its smaller

A A Parisian gunsmith's workshop at the end of the seventeenth century. On the left, the young apprentice learns from the master gunmaker. On the right, a journeyman removes the breech plug from a barrel. In the window hang pistols, guns, and holsters. From Nicolas Guérard, *Diverses Pièces d'Arquebuserie* (Paris, *c.* 1720).
B A silver-gilt trigger guard from a flintlock sporting gun which was made at Versailles, under Boutet, for King Charles IV of Spain, *c.* 1803.
C Two seventeenth-century shooters using matchlocks.

bore, enough powder and balls could be conveniently carried for long hunting excursions (and this had additional importance in a land where powder and lead were often hard to obtain). Moreover, it was accurate enough for squirrel shooting and powerful enough to kill deer or bears. Although it was developed chiefly in Pennsylvania, it became most famous as the "Kentucky rifle."

But during the early years of New World exploration and colonization, no *Jägers* had yet been brought to America, no light, double-barreled fowling pieces had yet been perfected, and the Pennsylvania/Kentucky rifle had not been developed. Some of the guns that first crossed the Atlantic were deadly on massed waterfowl and for jack-lighted deer, but few of them were much more effective than the long bow at moderate to long range. They were not much good, to cite an important example, for "still-hunting" deer—that is, moving through the forest silently and alertly in search of prey.

The Indian bows were vastly inferior to European and English long bows, which were already going out of use in the Old World, yet the Indian weapons had at least one advantage over the first firearms to arrive in America. Because the bow is nearly silent, if the first arrow misses, the animal will often remain still long enough for a second shot to be made.

The European crossbow was powerful and accurate but difficult to handle skillfully and, since a mechanical windlass with a series of pulleys or a gear-and-rack device (a "crannequin") was required to bend a really powerful crossbow, these arms were much slower to operate than a long bow. Moreover, powerful crossbows were costly and difficult to build. The simple bow, European or Indian, thus had hunting advantages that have been slighted by some historians.

The Indians, then, had rapid-fire "repeaters," while the Europeans were limited to single-shot guns and slow-loading crossbows. The Spanish in sixteenth-century Florida discovered that, once the Indians' initial awe of the "thunder sticks" had passed, their arrows were often more than a match for European weaponry.

This was particularly true in the American West before the arrival of repeating firearms in the nineteenth century. Riding the descendants of horses that had been introduced into New Spain or Mexico by the Spanish, the Plains Indian could loose off one arrow after another, while his white opponent struggled to prepare his muzzleloader for a second shot.

In hunting, the Western Indians used methods that would have been familiar to Stone Age Europeans. For thousands of years, at least two species of bison (the earlier, now extinct, form was larger) were driven off the edge of cliffs, just as the Europeans had done with the wild horse.

Before the horse was available to the Indians, they had only dogs to help them carry their belongings on sleds. With little mobility, because they traveled on foot, survival was of paramount importance, and hunting would have been only for food.

When the Plains Indians began to make use of the horse in earnest, at about the end of the eighteenth century, their lives were progressively revolutionized. Within hardly more than one hundred years, they had been overwhelmed by the Frontier but had first reached the apex of their development. With the horse came mobility and security from hunger, a refined system of warfare based on horse-stealing raids, and wide-ranging hunting, possibly partly for pleasure.

They now had the means of galloping alongside a rushing bison and of shooting it with bow and arrow. He who could do this, and speedily bring down the prey, was esteemed by his fellows as a great hunter.

Today, hunting buffalo in preserves with modern guns is held by many to be an unsporting contest, for the animals are slow, whereas on the Plains, where they were hunted on horseback, they were powerful, fast, and capable of turning on a rider and his horse and of killing both of them. Moreover, the abundance of prairie-dog holes added to the risks,

but the exhilaration of galloping over the Plains in the midst of a herd of buffalo was such that, in the period from the 1830s to the 1870s, Americans—and frequently European noblemen, too—traveled long distances to engage in it. This type of hunting had been begun by the Indians, who had, however, used only bows and arrows.

Most often, as a herd of bison milled or stampeded about them, these mounted sportsmen used pistols to bring down the great beasts. The American writer Washington Irving wielded a single-shot percussion pistol on such a hunt and afterward wrote of his experience in *A Tour on the Prairies.* The painter George Catlin depicted himself "running buffalo" with a Colt revolver—an obvious choice of arms, since Samuel Colt had commissioned the painting for advertising purposes. In 1837, Captain William Drummond Stewart, a wealthy and famous Scottish sportsman and explorer, who is now remembered chiefly as patron of the painter Alfred Jacob Miller, toured the Great Plains and the Rocky Mountains. On this journey Captain Stewart, too, rode among the bison with a single-shot percussion pistol.

In 1872, Grand Duke Alexis of Russia visited the United States as a diplomatic guest of President Ulysses S. Grant. One objective of his visit was the testing and purchase of .44-caliber Smith & Wesson revolvers for Russian army units. Like so many other wealthy Europeans, he longed to gallop among the thundering bison, and for a man of his rank, such a hunt was easy to arrange. He tested the revolvers by shooting bison with them. His companions on the hunt were Generals George A. Custer and Philip Sheridan. His guides were the celebrated Colonel "Buffalo Bill" Cody and "Texas Jack" Omohundro. Within about fifteen years, the buffalo had vanished from the Plains . . .

While western sport hunting, at least for whites, awaited the nineteenth century, eastern sport hunting developed as quickly as desire and technology allowed. The early Virginians, ever anxious to emulate the society of their mother country, were early devotees of "riding to the hounds." George Washington was one of the greatest enthusiasts of fox hunting.

America had, of course, also been blessed with a fantastic abundance of wildfowl. But as long as deer remained common, most hunters scorned smaller game. Still, in one region after another, it did not take long for deer to be overhunted to the point of nonexistence, for venison was a staple food. Virtually every effort to pass regulations was thwarted, for "game laws" were a vestige of English "tyranny," which the colonials believed they had left behind in the Old World.

When deer had became difficult or impossible to obtain, colonials looked to smaller game, and when they lived near large bodies of water, they soon discovered that, for a good part of the year, they might obtain more meat from ducks and geese than they formerly had from deer. In the 1630s, less than twenty years after Plymouth, Massachusetts, was founded, Edward Winslow, governor of the Plymouth colony, wrote about shooting waterfowl from blinds with heavy smoothbore muskets, probably mounted or rested when fired at sitting ducks.

Whether shooting upland birds or waterfowl, the most common American method well into the nineteenth century was to shoot the game sitting. Even after the double-barreled shotgun was introduced, one was expected to take the first shot on the water or on the ground, while the second shot—seen by many as almost a desperation effort—was taken as the game flushed.

The tardy adoption of "shooting flying" was the result of America's frontier heritage and a mentality that viewed hunting for sport, as distinct from hunting for meat, as an attempt to "put on airs," something that an egalitarian democracy despised. Given these and other anti-British traditions, it is hardly surprising that it took a long time for Americans to take to the "flying shooting" that had been known in Spain by the 1640s and, after the political turmoils of the intervening years, by the 1680s in

England. In *The Gentleman's Recreation*, published in England in 1686, the author Richard Blome notes: "It is now the Mode to shoot flying as being by Experience found the best and surest Way; for when your Game is on the Wing, it is more exposed to Danger; for if but one shot hits any Part of the Wings so expanded, it will occasion its Fall, altho' not to kill it: so that your Spaniel will soon be its Victor, and, if well disciplined to the Sport, will bring it to you."

Those Americans who wanted to learn the mysteries of shooting birds on the wing could have turned to *The Sportsman's Companion* (1783), which one hunting authority has called "the first real sporting book published in America." Written by an anonymous sportsman, probably a British officer stationed in what by then had been the colonies, it portrays the latest English methods of hunting wildfowl, gives hints on the use of pointers and retrievers, and even reminds the reader that he has a responsibility not to overexploit the wildlife resource.

Though Americans of that era seem to have had little interest in sporting literature, Englishmen were of exactly the opposite viewpoint. For example, Gaston de Foix's fourteenth-century *Livre de la Chasse*—which has been called "the first full-length work on hunting in Europe"—was translated into English between 1406 and 1413 by Edward, Second Duke of York. Called *The Master of Game*, it remained a standard work for centuries.

Other volumes also found ready acceptance. Among these are Sir Thomas Cockaine's *Short Treatise on Hunting* (1581), and Gervase Markham's *Country Contentments* (1615) and *Hunger's Prevention* (1621). With the rise of mercantilism, a relatively affluent middle class developed and embraced the hunt, no longer to obtain food but to emulate the aristocracy. Among such newly landed gentry, Markham's works were immensely popular.

But while Englishmen's interest in sport grew markedly in this period, their willingness to adopt superior technology and techniques stopped short of accepting the fact that gunmaking on the Continent, in Spain, France, and Germany, was far ahead of theirs. And, as we have seen, they were slow to practice "shooting flying," even after it had been in vogue for many years in Spain and France. Of course, one issue was related to the other, and poor guns made wingshooting less feasible.

Toward the end of the seventeenth century, they did enter the rather competitive business of gunmaking (with no little encouragement from their government, which took a natural interest in superior arms), and they did so with a rush. They imported the latest Continental inventions, and the great diarist Samuel Pepys, among others, wrote admiringly of European gadgets, including a couple of the earliest repeating firearms. In the eighteenth and early nineteenth centuries, the English not only took to the sport of "shooting flying" but became the finest makers of guns for the purpose. And the first truly successful percussion lock—the famous "scent-bottle" lock—was devised in 1807 by a Scottish clergyman, Alexander John Forsyth, who was an avid wildfowler.

It is odd that Great Britain, having become a nation of wingshooting enthusiasts as well as the source of the world's finest double-barreled shotguns in the nineteenth century—and of a people renowned for sportsmanship—continued to be the nation most devoted to shooting sitting ducks. This developed into a very specialized sport-within-a-sport, involving the use of enormous smoothbores, commonly called punt guns, mounted like cannon in the prows of duck boats. In the United States, punt gunning had become unfashionable among sportsmen by the late nineteenth century, although it was common among commercial market gunners for many years more, until it was stopped by law. In Great Britain, punt gunning has survived into the 1980s, with a small coterie of enthusiasts who feel that the sport lies partly in the handling of boat and gun, and partly in the challenge of paddling close enough to a large raft of waterfowl without alarming them into prema-

A self-spanning wheel-lock with a totally enclosed action, by Jacob Zimmerman, signed and dated 1646. The movement of the cock, holding the pyrites, compresses the spring which drives the wheel when the trigger is pressed.

ture flight. To be fair, this is not shooting at sitting ducks, for the ideal, most deadly shot is fired when the birds have risen a little off the water, making timing crucial.

While the Continent was moving ahead in gunmaking and techniques for wildfowl shooting, it was in a state of decadence when it came to big-game hunting. Not since the days of the Roman arena had Europe witnessed such joy in bloodletting. During the seventeenth and eighteenth centuries, in Spain, France, and what is now Germany, the most bizarre spectacles imaginable took place that had nothing to do with "hunting," though that term was used for them.

In one version of this pastime, deer were rounded up and herded down narrow alleys made of canvas screens and were wrestled to the ground and killed in front of spectators, many of whom were court ladies. In another version, deer were rounded up and forced through a "triumphal arch," down a hill, and into water, where they were shot by the "hunters." Ultimate decadence was achieved, however, when the game animals were dressed in bizarre clothing before being sent forward to be slaughtered.

Chapter 4

From the Golden Age to the Present

John F. Reiger

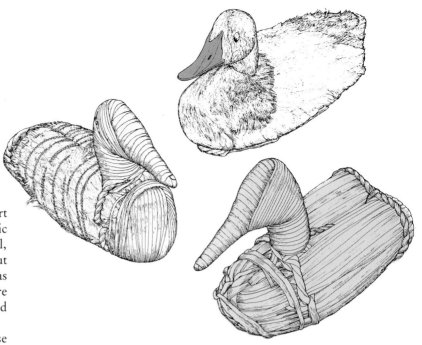

With the opening of the nineteenth century, great changes in sport occurred on both sides of the Atlantic. In Europe, the aristocratic liking for blood sports was eventually played down, as political, social, and philosophical ideas changed. In North America, new ideas about hunting began slowly to take root. For the first few decades, there was little sign that anything would ever change there. Game laws were abhorred as a vestige of Old World feudalism; every male believed he had the right to hunt all year long, and game was considered limitless.

One man would do more than anyone else to initiate a change in these sentiments. He was Henry William Herbert, an English aristocrat who arrived in the United States in the summer of 1831. He began writing sporting sketches in 1839 and continued until 1858, when he committed suicide.

Writing under the pseudonym of Frank Forester, he introduced into the United States gentlemanly concepts that may be called the code of the sportsman. Reading books like *Frank Forester's Field Sports* (1849), *American Game in Its Seasons* (1853), and *The Complete Manual for Young Sportsmen* (1856), American hunters learned that there was only one correct way to take game and that all other methods were "common," or even immoral. The basic idea was "fair play"—the game must be given a reasonable chance to escape; otherwise, no real sport was possible. Just as importantly, a "true sportsman" must hunt for esthetic reasons and not for meat or economic profit.

What Dame Julians Barnes and Izaak Walton had been to English angling, Herbert was to American hunting. He became the model for the rising generation of American sportsmen. And not the least of his accomplishments was to drive a wedge between sport and commercial hunters.

No code of any sportsman restrained the latter group. The sale of game has always been a part of European hunting, but there the game is sold by the owners or lessees of the hunting land, who are also the owners of the game and are responsible for maintaining it as a renewable resource. Retailing, at least in Great Britain, is also strictly licensed. It is in their own interest to prevent the depletion of wildlife. The marketing of game in Europe, therefore, has never encouraged the wholesale destruction perpetrated by the "market gunners" of nineteenth-century America.

The professional hunters argued, with some justice, that they were resented simply because they were better at taking game than the "amateurs." In any case, their argument continued, "fashion" demanded unlimited slaughter. If they did not kill and sell the game to the restaurants, hotels, and markets, someone else would. As if to encourage them, a writer in the popular, multi-volume *Cabinet of Natural History and American Rural Sports* observed in the early 1830s: "The Canvasback [duck], in the rich juicy tenderness of its flesh, and its delicacy and flavour, stands unrivalled by the whole of its tribe, in this or perhaps any other quarter of the world ... At our public dinners, hotels, and particular entertainments, the Canvas-backs are universal favourites. They not only grace but dignify the table, and their very name conveys to

Decoy making has a long history in North America. (Above) Three decoys, found in 1911 in Nevada; they were made well over a thousand years ago by the Tule Eater Indians, ancestors of the Northern Paiutes. Two of the decoys are made of tule reeds, and the third is a canvasback's head, skin, and feathers mounted over tule reeds. (Center) Goose hunters in a pit blind, using flat, painted decoys. By Charles A. Zimmerman, nineteenth century. (Below) The frame for a modern goose decoy.

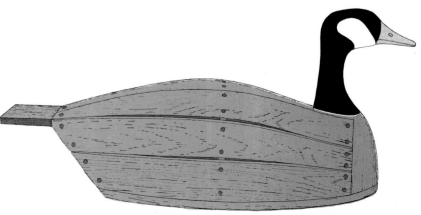

the imagination of the eager epicure, the most comfortable and exhilarating ideas. Hence on such occasions, it has not been uncommon to pay from one to three dollars a pair for these Ducks; and, indeed, at such times, if they can they must be had, whatever may be the price."

In the early part of the nineteenth century, both sportsmen and market gunners shot waterfowl such as canvasbacks from blinds, located on the end of points far out in tidal bays and rivers. Decoys were rare or unknown at first. As time went by, decoys, both live and wooden, came into wider use. While one authority after another has claimed that the employment of wooden decoys was copied from the Indians, no real proof has been offered to document this assertion. Archeologists have found cleverly made Indian decoys thousands of years old. These were generally fashioned of woven and bound reeds, and one surviving specimen has part of a duck's skin and plumage stretched over it. Decoys were seldom if ever used in Europe, but neither were they in wide use by Indians in the nineteenth century. Perhaps their development by American hunters arose out of the long practice of keeping "wing-tipped" (shot, but only slightly crippled) birds as barnyard fowl and live decoys. In order to "round out" a flock of tethered, captive birds, wooden dummies were anchored alongside. Wooden birds required far less care than live ones.

Though wooden decoys were developed independently in Scandinavia for hunting species (scoters, goldeneyes, and old-squaws) that were hunted also on the western side of the Atlantic, the folk art of the decoy achieved its highest development by far in the United States and southeastern Canada. Often a single hunter might use several hundred diving-duck decoys in conjunction with a "sink-box" (also called a "battery"). The latter looked something like a coffin with its top off. With weighted "wings" to keep the water from coming in, and anchored out in a calm sound, the device would be almost invisible to incoming waterfowl, which habitually fly low over the water when traveling in their feeding areas. With decoys completely surrounding the "box," and the hunter lying back with just his eyes peering over the edge, the ducks witnessed the incredible sight of a man doing a "sit-up" in ten feet of water as he fired at them from virtually point-blank range.

Sink-boxes proved disastrous for waterfowl populations because they led to huge bags of birds wherever they were used, and they were used in virtually every major waterfowl area along the Atlantic coast.

In Europe, duck traps were used instead. Known, interestingly enough, as "decoys," these ancient traps came in various shapes, but their general form was a huge netted funnel with the end closed off and the mouth situated in a baited pond or marsh. If the trap was of the kind used since the Middle Ages on the North Sea and Baltic coasts, the game was attracted by live decoy ducks and gently herded into the pipe by a slowly swimming dog. In England, the technique was to entice the birds inside the tunnel with a reddish-colored dog similar to a fox, and trained to appear and disappear in sight of the ducks. They became curious and followed it.

This use of a brightly colored dog with the English decoys probably has an evolutionary relationship to another hunting practice called "hunting with a red dog" in Europe and "tolling" in Canada and the United States. The dog is trained to scamper back and forth on a beach in sight of rafted ducks. Curious, they swim close enough to shore to be shot by hunters in blinds. Before about 1840, when sink-boxes were introduced into the Chesapeake Bay area by New York gunners, tolling had been one of the most popular methods for taking canvasbacks and other diving ducks. Gradually, the practice died out in the South but was still common in Nova Scotia as late as the 1930s.

By the last third of the nineteenth century, affluent sportsmen on both sides of the Atlantic were entering a "golden age" of hunting. New breechloading double-barreled shotguns had replaced the old muz-zleloaders, and repeating rifles had supplanted the muzzleloading rifle and rifled musket, at least for small and medium game. Towards the end of the century, repeating shotguns would appear in America, where they were eagerly adopted, particularly by market hunters. The English and many continental Europeans, however, still seem to believe that a gun firing more than two shots is not quite sporting, and repeaters have never been popular on the eastern side of the Atlantic.

Advances in gunmaking (and ammunition) combined with new developments in transportation and communications to present a unique opportunity to sportsmen of the period 1870–1914. These were the years of the New Imperialism, when European countries were struggling with one another to occupy every last blank spot on the map, and the West was being won. The "natives" were generally docile, the ecosystems as yet relatively undamaged, and the shooting unlimited for the hunter who had the money to outfit an expedition into the wilds.

When one thinks of big-game hunting in these years, the first place that usually comes to mind is sub-Saharan Africa. Because the Boer farmers had trekked into the interior by the 1840s, the southern portion of the continent was the first to feel the unrelenting hand of the hunter. By the 1870s, much of the game had been killed off. The Boers wanted meat, protection for their crops and stock, and skins, which found a ready market in Europe. Some also killed elephants for ivory.

In the early 1870s, however, game was still abundant over the rest of the African continent. The Van Zyl family, for example, killed a herd of over one hundred elephants in one day near Lake Ngami! Early in the nineteenth century, the Boers were able to stop elephants with sixteen-pound smoothbores loaded with 4-ounce balls backed by seventeen drams of black powder. Later, breechloading double-barreled rifles were introduced that made elephant hunting somewhat less hazardous.

If sportsmen in Africa, and Asia as well, were unmindful of game depletion, it must be said in fairness to them that the game seemed limitless, and also that, quite often, they were equally unmindful of the danger to themselves. Just as they had enjoyed "running buffalo" in North America, they enjoyed facing charging African and Asian game at close quarters, sometimes with surprisingly small arms. A "howdah" pistol was, for instance, developed for shooting Indian tigers from the back of an elephant.

As with the slaughter taking place on the Western Plains of the United States in the same period, there seemed to be little restraint on the part of the hunters. Visiting Europeans and Englishmen always spoke in the most glowing terms of enormous bags. What Sir John Willoughby and Sir Robert Harvey started in Kenya in the 1880s continued until World War 1. "A continuous procession," as one writer described it, of wealthy sportsmen and sportswomen came to East Africa in quest of limitless shooting and trophy heads. Soon it was East Africa's turn to witness the sad decline of its great herds, just as South Africa had done years before. By 1910, former big-game hunters were lamenting the barren, monotonous wastes, stretching mile after mile, that once teemed with life.

While Africa was *the* place to go for a fashionable hunt in the period 1870–1914, other areas also won adherents. Australia and New Zealand had little to offer in the way of native big game, but North America was still popular. And for many, there was no area quite so exotic and appealing as the Far East.

Though the European presence in India goes back to the Portuguese in the sixteenth century, the first book on sport in that part of the world was Captain Thomas Williamson's *Oriental Field Sports* (1807). In it, the British officer describes the hunting in Bengal in the last twenty years of the eighteenth century. The book documents the devotion of Indian princes to the chase and their hunting methods, later to be employed by Western sportsmen in pursuing the incredible diversity of game available in India.

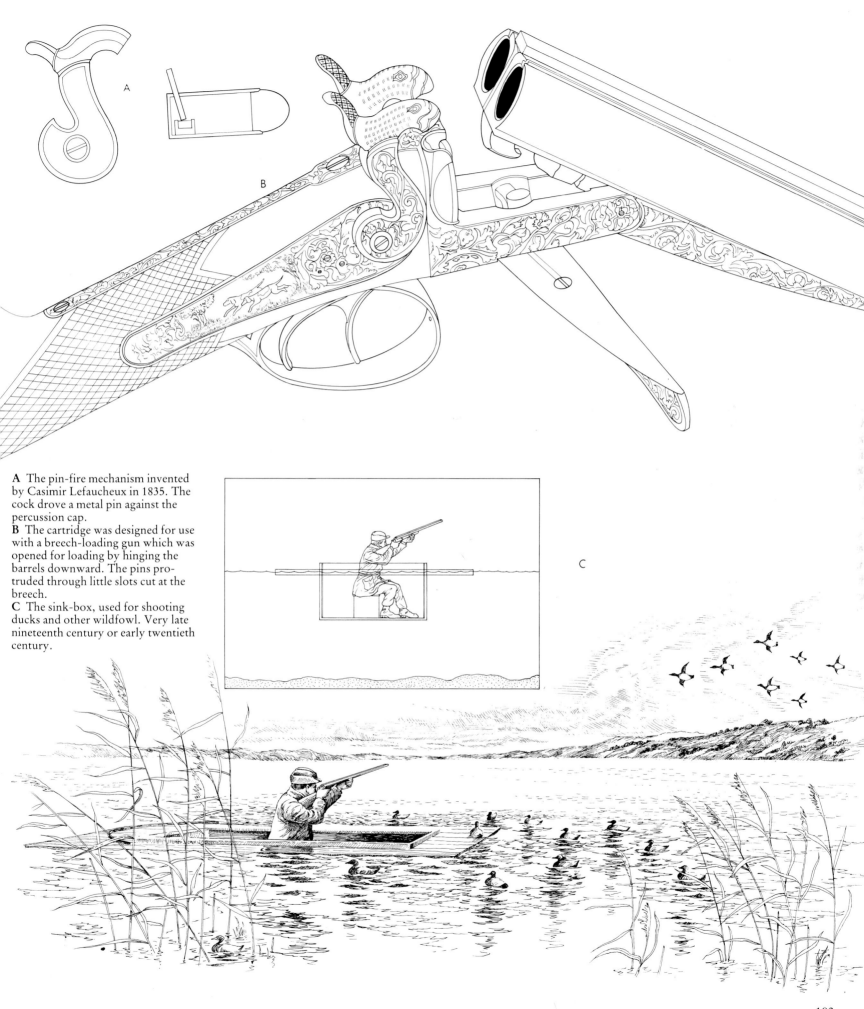

A The pin-fire mechanism invented by Casimir Lefaucheux in 1835. The cock drove a metal pin against the percussion cap.
B The cartridge was designed for use with a breech-loading gun which was opened for loading by hinging the barrels downward. The pins protruded through little slots cut at the breech.
C The sink-box, used for shooting ducks and other wildfowl. Very late nineteenth century or early twentieth century.

Like the earlier Kublai Khan, the Eastern aristocracy liked hunting spectacles. Williamson cites, for example, the use of two or three thousand trained elephants accompanying a prince on a hunt!

The British captain also discusses bear and boar hunting with lances, the hunters usually being mounted on horseback—another instance of the sportsman courting danger (and, perhaps, unconsciously making contact with his Stone Age heritage). One authority who has analyzed Williamson's work believes that the nineteenth-century English sport of "pig sticking" developed when bears proved to be too scarce to hunt with any certain success of finding the quarry. Thus, the hunters transferred the method of lancing bears to the more common wild boars. Certainly there was nothing "decadent" about facing the tusks of a boar armed only with a lance. In a fair number of cases, the hunter was dismounted and hurt.

It was only natural that coursing, too, would find a place in nineteenth-century India. After all, coursing was popular for hares in Europe, emu in Australia, and jackrabbits in the western United States. The game in India was hare, gazelle, and jackal, and was coursed with greyhounds.

Other small game included the many bird species, even peacock. These were frequently shot by sportsmen over English pointers brought especially for that purpose!

Of course, the most glamorous and dangerous game were the large mammals: elephant, tiger, leopard, and even rhinoceros. The subconti-nent had these and many others in good numbers until well into this century. Unlike that of Africa—with its plains and savannas—much of the game country of India was thick rain forest, where the wildlife was difficult to approach. Game, therefore, was not as quickly overexploited.

The favorite way to hunt tigers, until rather recently, was to have beaters drive the game toward the hunter, who sat in a howdah, a partly enclosed platform mounted on an elephant's back. Tigers have killed and eaten enough Indians over the centuries to indicate that, even unpro-voked, they are among the world's most dangerous beasts. One that was enraged enough to leap up into the howdah must have provided exhilarating moments for the tiger hunter.

With the exception of improved weaponry and, perhaps, the introduc-tion of certain breeds of hunting dog, eighteenth-century hunting methods remained unchanged into the twentieth century. Times, how-ever, were rapidly changing, not just for India, but for Europe and the Americas as well. Human population explosions, industrial expansion, and independence movements were all undercutting the unique set of circumstances that had created the "golden age" of hunting in the late nineteenth and early twentieth centuries. In one area of the world after another, frantic, last-minute efforts would be made to manage what little wildlife was left; but in much of the "third world," the efforts seem to have been in vain. Only in Great Britain and parts of Europe and North America, where strict regulations were passed and enforced, have species been restored to the abundance of the "golden age."

IV Reference

Hunter's Lexicon

Jerome Knap
Wilson Stephens

Action: The breech mechanism of a gun, by means of which it is loaded and which secures the cartridge in the chamber, preventing the cartridge from discharging to the rear. Also, a field-trial term describing the manner in which a dog moves in the field; the British term is "style."

Afon: A stream in Wales.

Aperture Sight: See **Sights**.

Autoloader: See **Semiautomatic**.

Automatic: Any firearm which continues to fire, to the extent of the capacity of its magazine, so long as the trigger is depressed. Sometimes erroneously applied to semiautomatic firearms.

Automatic Safety: See **Safety**.

Backing: An expression of a dog's pointing instinct, when a dog comes to point at sight of another dog's point, to "back" him, or "honor" his point.

Balance: In theory, the balance is that point between butt and muzzle where a gun balances when rested on a fulcrum. A gun balances properly when the point of balance is midway between the points where the hands naturally hold the gun in shooting. However, this is not the common understanding of the term. In most cases, balance is understood to mean the feel it gives the shooter in handling the gun—that is, whether correctly balanced or either muzzle-light or muzzle-heavy.

Ballistics: The theory of the motion of projectiles. The shooter loosely considers "ballistics" to mean data relative to the velocity, energy, trajectory, and penetration of a cartridge, and sometimes to related factors such as chamber pressure and a powder's burning characteristics.

Barrens: Flat wasteland with low, stunted vegetation. Also, a broad, flat marsh.

Bay: Second point of antlers, after the brow and before the tray; sometimes spelt "bey."

Bead: See **Sights**.

Beat (n): An area to be beaten or driven to flush out game.

Beat (v): To beat bushes etc., to drive out game.

Beater (n): One who beats, in order to send the game over the shooters at a covert shoot or grouse drive.

Beck: A stream in northern England.

Bed: Where big game—or even hares or rabbits—have been sleeping or resting. Another term for a rabbit or hare bed is "form."

Belted Cartridge: A cartridge, primarily of the heavy-caliber, high-velocity type, which is rimless but has a belt around the base.

Belton: A type of color formed in English setters when two colors blend so closely as to lose individual identity. Blue belton is a combination of black and white; orange belton a combination of orange and white.

Bench Rest: A wooden shooting bench, heavily constructed and firmly placed, with suitable "rest" for the muzzle or barrel, at which the shooter may sit to engage in accuracy tests of the firearm.

Bevy: A group of game birds, such as quail, generally a brood.

Big-bore: A rather loose adjective, normally applied in North America to rifles of calibers larger than .25, but applied in some countries only to much larger calibers. Also, large-bore.

Blind: A natural or man-made hiding place from which a hunter shoots ducks, turkeys, or other game. The British term is "hide."

Block: Colloquial word for a duck decoy.

Blowback: Automatic or semiautomatic action in which extraction, ejection, and reloading are accomplished by means of the force exerted rearward by the gas of the fired cartridge.

Blowdown: A thick tangle of fallen trees and brush, usually the result of severe winds.

Blown Primer: A cartridge case in which the primer was blown out during firing. Can cause serious injury, even blindness, to the shooter; one good argument for use of shooting glasses.

Bluebird Weather: Sunny, windless conditions which are the bane of the wildfowler's existence, as waterfowl normally do not move in such weather or else fly very high.

Boat-tail Bullet: A bullet with a tapered rear end designed to obtain greater efficiency at longer ranges.

Bore: The inside of the barrel of a shotgun, rifle, revolver, or pistol, the diameter of which is the caliber or gauge of the weapon. The term is also a synonym for "gauge" of a shotgun.

Brace: Standard term for two quail, partidge, pheasant, grouse, hares, or dogs.

Breech: The base (as opposed to the muzzle) of a gun barrel; the rear portion of the barrel, which, in a modern rifle, is chambered to hold the cartridge.

Breeding: The ancestry of a dog.

Brocket: A male red deer in his third year.

Broken: Term for a finished, completely trained bird dog.

Brood: All young together born or hatched by one female. See **Bevy** and **Covey**.

Brow: The first, or brow, point of antlers.

Browse: Branches of trees, small saplings, or low brush, which serve as food for members of the deer family and other ruminants.

Brush-cutter: A bullet, usually of large caliber and considerable weight, having enough velocity and weight to continue its original course without being deflected by light brush.

Brush Gun: A rifle or shotgun with a barrel shorter than average, designed for ease of movement through heavy brush.

Buck: American term for the male of various species, including antelope, goat, deer, and rabbit; in Britain, of non-native deer imported to Britain, and of the rabbit. Also, an accessory used in teaching retrieving, sometimes called a retrieving dummy.

Buckshot: Large lead or alloy shot used in shotgun shells, principally for big game such as deer.

Buffer: A biological term used to designate small forms of animal life upon which predators will feed, thus reducing the mortality of game. When enough "buffers" are present, predators eat fewer game animals.

Bugle: The sound a bull elk (wapiti) makes during the rutting (breeding) season to advertise his presence to the females and to issue challenges to the other bulls. The British term is "roaring" for stags of European red deer. In some regions, "bugling" is also used to describe the cries of hounds.

Bump: Slang for accidental flushing of game birds by a pointing dog.

Burn: An area which has been burned over by a forest fire; also, a stream in Scotland.

Burst: Generally, the first part of the run when hounds are close upon the fox; any fast part of a chase.

Butt (1): The rear part of a gun stock from the grip area rearward.

Butt (2): Camouflaged embrasure in which a shooter waits for the birds at a grouse drive. Also, the backing behind a target that stops the bullets.

Butt Plate: The metal, plastic, or hard-rubber plate covering the rear of a gunstock, usually checkered or corrugated to prevent slipping. See **Recoil Pad** or **Stock.**

Calf: Young, either sex, of the red deer until a year old.

Caliber: The diameter of the bore of a rifled arm in hundredths of an inch or in millimeters, usually measured from land to land (raised portion between grooves), which gives the true diameter of the bore prior to the cutting of grooves.

Caller: A hunter who does the calling when hunting ducks, geese, or turkeys, or other game.

Cape: The hide or pelage covering the head, neck, and foreshoulders of a game animal, often removed for mounting as a trophy. The British term is headskin.

Carbine: A short-barreled rifle, normally much lighter in weight than a standard rifle.

Carrier: The mechanism in a magazine or repeating firearm (other than a revolver) which carries the shell or cartridge from the magazine into a position to be pushed into the chamber by the closing of the breechbolt.

Carry the Line: When hounds are following the scent, they are "carrying the line."

Cast: The spreading out, or reaching out, of a pointing dog in search of game or of hounds in search of a scent. Also, in archery, the speed with which the bow will throw an arrow. Also, in falconry, a group or flight of hawks.

Centerfire: A cartridge of which the primer is contained in a pocket in the center of the cartridge base.

Chalk: White excreta of a woodcock, indicating the presence of birds in a covert.

Chamber: The enlarged portion of the gun barrel at the breech, in which the cartridge fits when in position for firing.

Charge: Load of powder and/or shot in a shotshell, or the load of powder in a muzzle-loading gun. Also, an old command, still occasionally used, to a hunting dog to lie down; it derives from the time when gun dogs were required to lie down while the guns were charged.

Cheeper: Game bird too young to be shot.

Chilled Shot: Shot containing a greater percentage of antimony than soft lead. All shot except buckshot and steel shot is dropped from a tower. Buckshot of the large sizes is cast, as are single balls.

Choke: The constriction in the muzzle of a shotgun bore by means of which control is exerted upon the shot charge in order to throw its pellets into a definite area of predetermined concentration. Degree of choke is measured by the approximate percentage of pellets in a shot charge, which hit within a 30-inch circle at 40 yards. The following table gives the accepted percentages obtained with various chokes:

Full Choke..65 % minimum
Improved Modified...60–70 %
Modified...50–65 %
Improved Cylinder ....35–50 %
Cylinder ....25–35 %

Choke Constriction: The amount of constriction at the muzzle of various gauges, which produces choke, is as follows:

Gauge	Full Choke		Modified Choke		Improved Cylinder		Cylinder	
	inch	mm	inch	mm	inch	mm	inch	mm
10	.035	.889	.017	.432	.007	.178	0	0
12	.030	.762	.015	.381	.006	.152	0	0
16	.024	.610	.012	.305	.005	.127	0	0
20	.021	.533	.010	.254	.004	.102	0	0
28	.017	.432	.008	.203	.003	.076	0	0

Clip: Detachable magazine of a rifle or a pistol. A metal container designed to contain a given number of cartridges for a repeating rifle.

Cock (n): Male bird.

Cock (v): Make ready a firearm for firing by pulling back the hammer or firing pin to full cock. A firearm with a visible hammer usually has half-cock and full-cock positions.

Cold Line: The faint scent of the quarry.

Comb: The upper and forward edge of a gunstock against which the shooter rests his cheek.

Conseil International De La Chasse: An organization comprising members from various European countries, which assumes responsibility for the classification and measurement system employed in recording trophies of European big game.

Coon: A colloquialism for raccoon.

Cope: Muzzle for a ferret.

Couple: Two woodcock, snipe, waterfowl, shorebirds, or rabbits. Also used to describe two hounds.

Course: In fox hunting, to run by sight and not by nose. Also, the territory to be covered in a field trial for bird dogs and spaniels.

Cover: Trees, undergrowth, grass, or reeds in which game may lie. A place to be hunted.

Covert: In fox hunting, a place where fox may be found. Also, woodland. Also, the name for a place where any game may be found. Same as cover.

Covert-shoot: Pheasant shooting in which the shooters wait in line outside woodland from which the birds are driven by beaters.

Coverts: The wing feathers which cover the base of the flight feathers.

Covey: A group of game birds such as quail; a bevy. Also, a British term for a family group of grouse or partridge, generally four to sixteen birds.

Crimp: That portion of a cartridge case or shotshell, which is turned inward to grip the bullet or to hold the end wad in place, respectively.

Cripple: A game bird that has been shot down but not killed. This term is normally employed in duck shooting. (In upland shooting, the term "winged" is more often used.)

Cross Hairs: The cross-hair reticule or aiming device in a telescopic sight on a rifle. Wire or nylon is now used instead of hair.

Cry: The voice of a hound. The cry varies during the chase. By its tone, the other hounds can tell how strong the scent is and how sure the line is.

Dancing Ground: An area where such birds as prairie chicken, sharptail grouse, sage grouse, and black grouse perform their courtship dances in the spring.

Doe: Female of fallow, roe, or imported deer, and of the hare or rabbit.

Dogging: The shooting of grouse or partidges over pointers or setters.

Double: Any shotgun with two barrels, whether the side-by-side type or the over-and-under. Also, when a fox, raccoon, or other game animal turns back on his course to elude hounds.

Drag: Scent left by a fox as he returns to his den; or an artificial trail made by dragging a scented bag for hounds to follow.

Dram: Unit of weight, which is the equivalent of 27.5 grains. There are 256 drams in one pound avoirdupois (454 g).

Dram Equivalent: In the early days of black-powder shotshells, the powder charge was measured in drams. Dram for dram, today's smokeless powder is more powerful. The term "3 dram equivalent" means that the amount of smokeless powder used produces the same shot velocity as would 3 drams of black powder.

Drift: Deviation of any projectile, bullet, or arrow from the plane of its departure, caused by wind. Also, the deviation of the projectile from the plane of departure due to rotation. In all sporting firearms, the drift from the plane of departure due to rotation is so slight as to be of no consequence.

Drive (v): To move game toward the shooters.

Drive (n): A self-contained operation during a day's shooting in which the shooters remain stationary while game is driven from a particular direction.

Driven Game: Birds which are moved toward the shooters by beaters.

Driving: Method of hunting in which the hunters are divided into two groups. One group moves to an area to take up stands or watches covering a wide terrain; the other group moves toward the first, making sufficient noise to drive the game toward the group on watches. The individuals on watch are termed "standers" and those driving the game "drivers," or in Britain, "beaters."

Drop: Distance below the line of sight of a rifle or shotgun from an extension of this line to the comb and to the heel of the stock. See **Drop at Comb** and **Drop at Heel.**

Drop at Comb: Vertical distance between the prolonged line of sight and the point of the comb. The drop and thickness of the comb are the most important dimensions in the stock of a shotgun or rifle. They are affected by the drop at heel. If the dimensions are correct, the eye is guided into and held steadily in the line of aim. For hunting purposes, the best standard drop at comb on both rifles and shotguns is $1\frac{1}{4}$ to $1\frac{5}{8}$ inches (3.8–4.1 cm). Drop differs for target shooting. Ideal stock dimensions for field or target shooting are attained only by custom fitting.

Drop at Heel: The vertical distance between the prolonged line of sight and the heel of the butt. The amount of drop varies, depending upon the ideas and build of the shooter. Most shotgun hunters require a drop of about $2\frac{1}{4}$ inches (6.4 cm).

Earth: The hole of some burrowing animal, such as a woodchuck, appropriated by a fox. Also, the den.

Eclipse Plumage: The plumage of a male bird before the time when he takes on his full breeding plumage.

Ejector: Mechanism which ejects an empty case or loaded cartridge from a gun after it has been withdrawn, or partly withdrawn, from the chamber by the extractor. In a double-barreled shotgun, ejector often means extractor; "selective ejection" means automatic ejection of the fired shell only and is otherwise called automatic ejection.

Ejector Hammers: In a double-barreled shotgun, the driving pistons which eject the fired shells.

Elevation: The angle which the rear sight must be raised or lowered to compensate for the trajectory of the bullet and ensure the desired point of impact at different ranges.

Exotic: Any game bird or animal which has been imported.

Extractor: The hooked device which draws the cartridge out of the chamber when the breech mechanism is opened.

Fault: A check or interruption in a run by hounds caused by loss of scent.

Fawn: Offspring of the year of any deer other than red deer.

Field Dressing: The minimum dressing-out of a game animal in the field, merely enough to ensure preservation of the meat and the trophy, means usually the removing of the entrails and visceral organs.

Firing Pin: The pointed nose of the hammer of a firearm or the separate pin or plunger which, actuated by the hammer or the mainspring, dents the primer, thus firing the cartridge.

Firelighting: See **Jacklighting.**

Flag: The tail of a whitetail deer. Also, the long hair on a setter's tail.

Flat Trajectory: A term used to describe the low trajectory of high-velocity bullets which travel for a long distance over a flatter arc than other bullets. Scientifically an incorrect term, for no trajectory is truly flat. See also **Trajectory.**

Flighting: Ambushing duck or pigeon at their roosts or feeding grounds.

Fling: A period of aimless running before an enthusiastic bird dog settles to hunting.

Flush (n): The act of a questing dog putting game birds into the air, or an animal on foot.

Flushing Wild: Rise of game birds which have not been obviously disturbed, or birds that have been flushed out of shotgun range.

Flyway: Migration route of birds between breeding and wintering grounds. Also, the route waterfowl use between feeding and roosting areas.

Forearm: Synonymous with fore-end, although some use "forearm" when the butt stock and foregrip are separate pieces. See **Fore-end.**

Fore-end: Portion of the wooden gunstock forward of the receiver and under the barrel.

Forest: Open mountains, devoid of trees, on which stags are stalked in Scotland.

Fresh Line: Opposite of "cold line"— a fresh, or "hot," scent of game pursued by hounds.

Fur: All four-legged quarry.

Gaggle: A flock of geese. An old British term.

Game: In British law, pheasants, all partidges, all grouse, woodcock and snipe; by custom, also deer and hares.

Gang: A flock of brant. Also, an old British term for a group of European elk (moose).

Gas-operated: Said of a semiautomatic firearm which utilizes the gases generated by the powder combustion, before the bullet emerges from the muzzle, to operate a piston which extracts, ejects, and reloads the arm to the extent of the number of rounds in the magazine.

Gauge: The bore size of a shotgun. The number of the gauge has no relation to the linear measurement of the bore. Gauge is determined by the number of equal spheres, each of which exactly fits the barrel of the gun, which may be obtained from 1 lb (454 g) of lead. For example, a 12-gauge gun has a bore diameter the same as one of the twelve identically-sized spheres which can be made from a pound of lead. See **Bore.**

Gauge Measurements: The bore diameters of various gauges are as follows:

10 gauge	.775 inches (19 · 69 mm)
12 gauge	.725 inches (18 · 42 mm)
16 gauge	.662 inches (16 · 81 mm)
20 gauge	.615 inches (15 · 62 mm)
28 gauge	.550 inches (13 · 97 mm)
.410 gauge	.410 inches (10 · 41 mm)

Ghillie: Attendant, usually in charge of the pony, who accompanies a stalking party in Scotland. Also, an attendant on a fisherman.

Glass (v): To scan terrain with binoculars or telescope to locate game.

Grain: Abbreviated gr. Weight measurement. One ounce equals 437.5 gr. There are 7,000 gr in 1 lb (454 grams). In reference to gunstocks, grain indicates the direction of the fibers on the surface of the stock.

Gralloch (v): To field dress big-game animals immediately after shooting by removing the viscera and entrails. See **Field Dressing.**

Gram: Abbreviated g. Weight measurement. The equivalent of 15.43 grains.

Graze: Grasses, weeds, and similar low growths upon which deer and other ruminants feed.

Grip: That part of the stock of a rifle or shotgun which is grasped by the trigger hand when firing the gun. The two most common types of grips are the "pistol grip" and the "straight grip" found on some double-barreled shotguns.

Group: A series of shots fired at a target with a constant sight setting and point of aim. The diameter of the group is measured from the centers of the outer holes.

Group Diameter: The distance between centers of the two shots most widely separated in a group.

Gun: Any smooth-bore weapon projecting a charge of pellets; see also **Rifle.** Also, a participant in a British shooting party, as distinct from a helper or spectator.

Hair Trigger: A trigger requiring extremely light pressure for the release of the hammer.

Hammer: That part of a firearm, actuated by the mainspring and controlled by the trigger, which strikes either the cartridge rim or primer, or strikes and drives forward the firing pin so that it indents the primer or rim of the cartridge, to discharge the cartridge.

Hammerless: Of firearms having the hammer concealed within the breech mechanism.

Handgun: A firearm that is normally fired with one hand. A pistol or revolver.

Handloads: Cartridges loaded by hand for precision shooting, as opposed to commercial or "factory loads."

Hang-fire: Delayed ignition of the powder in a cartridge after the hammer has fallen and the primer has been struck.

Hard-mouthed: Of a dog that chews or crushes birds when retrieving.

Hart: The male deer. Usually used to refer to male red deer in Britain. A stag.

Head (n): The antlers of a deer, of any species and either sex.

Head (v): For a shooter to take post in advance of others to intercept birds flushing out of range of the rest.

Headspace: The space between the head of the bolt or breechblock and the base of the cartridge. Excessive headspace is exceedingly dangerous and can result in the bursting of the receiver.

Headstamp: The letters or number, or both, on the base of a cartridge.

Heel (n): Upper part of the butt of a shotgun or rifle. Also, a command to a dog to walk quietly beside or at the heel of the person giving the order.

Hide: Camouflaged embrasure in which a shooter waits for duck or pigeon. See **Blind.** Also, the skin of an animal.

High-base Shell: A shotgun shell furnished with high inside base wad, approximately $\frac{3}{4}$ inch (19 mm) thick before forming.

High-brass Shell: High-velocity shotgun shell on which the brass base extends a considerable distance up the plastic tube.

High Intensity: A term associated with a rifle or cartridge having a velocity of more than 2,500 foot-seconds (762 m/seconds).

High Power: A term associated with a rifle or cartridge having a velocity of more than 2,000 foot-seconds (609 m/seconds).

Hind: The female of the red deer.

Hochstand (Ger.): The seat at tree-top height from which deer are shot in woodland.

Hull: Empty cartridge or shell.

Hummle: A mature red deer stag which has grown no antlers.

Hunting: In British usage, the pursuit by a pack of hounds of ground quarry (fox, deer, hare) with followers mounted or on foot; gun sport is "shooting" in British idiom.

Imperial Bull: A bull elk (wapiti) that has seven points on each antler; a relatively rare and highly desirable trophy. Also, imperial stag in the case of European red deer.

Iron Sight: See **Sights.**

Jack: The male of the hare.

Jacklighting: The illegal practice of shooting game at night with the help of artificial light, which is reflected by the eyes of the game. Synonymous with firelighting.

Jump-shooting: A method of duck hunting in which the hunter stealthily approaches ducks by boat, or by stalking toward water, until within range and then flushes them.

Juvenile: A bird which, though having attained full growth, has not attained full adult characteristics or plumage. See also **Cheeper.**

Kentucky Windage: A term used by American riflemen to describe the process of "holding off" to the left or right of a target to allow for the effect of the wind on the bullet, but making no adjustment in the sight setting.

Knobber: Male red deer in his second year.

Lead (n): Term used to designate the distance it is necessary to hold ahead of any bird or animal to compensate for its speed of movement and the time required for the bullet or hot charge to reach it. The British term is forward allowance.

Lead (v): To cause a dog to follow under restraint, by means of a cord or leather thong attached to the dog's collar.

Leash: A group of three quail, partridge, pheasant, grouse, or hares. Also, a cord to lead a dog, a dog lead.

Length of Stock: The distance in a straight line from the center of the trigger to a point midway between the heel and toe of the buttplate, on the surface of the plate. Required stock length depends upon the build of the shooter, men of short stature or short arms requiring short stocks. The standard length for hunting arms is 14 inches (35.6 cm) for shotguns and $13\frac{1}{2}$ inches (34.3 cm) for rifles. Also called length of pull.

Line: The track or trail of an animal indicated by the scent the hounds are following. Also, the shooters deployed at a formal shoot, called "the line."

Line of Sight: The straight line between the eye of the shooter and the target. See **Trajectory.**

Line-running: Of a dog that casts in straight lines rather than hunts in places where birds are usually found.

Line Shooting: A form of scoter (sea duck) shooting along the North American Atlantic coast, in which several boats line up across a known scoter flyway to shoot at the birds as they fly past.

Live Weight: The computed or estimated weight of a game animal before it is dressed out.

Loader: Attendant who holds and re-loads the second weapon when a shooter uses two guns at a covert shoot where many birds are expected.

Loch: A lake in Scotland (also lough (Ireland) and llyn (Wales).

Lock: The combination of hammer, firing pin, sear, mainspring, and trigger which serves to discharge the cartridge when the trigger is pulled.

Lock Time: The time elapsed between the release of the hammer by the sear and the impact of the firing pin on the primer. Also called lock speed.

Lubrication of Bullets: Most lead bullets have to be lubricated with grease or wax on their surface or in their grooves to prevent leading the bore. Outside-lubricated cartridges have the lubricant placed on the surface of the bullet outside the case. Inside-lubricated bullets have the lubricant in grooves or cannelures on the bullet where it is covered by the neck of the case.

Lug: In a break-down, breech-loading shotgun or rifle, a lug on the barrel secures the barrel to the frame. Lugs on the front of a bolt or breechblock which rotate into slots to lock the action for firing are termed locking lugs.

Magazine: The tube or box which holds cartridges or shells in reserve for mechanical insertion into the chamber of a repeating firearm.

Magazine Plug: Plug or dowel placed inside or against the magazine spring of a slide-action or semiautomatic shotgun to limit the capacity of the magazine in order to comply with the law. (In the United States, waterfowlers may have no more than three shells in their guns; some individual states limit magazine capacity for other game.)

Mark: A call used to warn another shooter of the flushing or approach of a game bird. The term is often accompanied by a direction: "mark right" or "mark left."

Mark Down: To use some terrain feature to mark the location of a fallen game bird in order to facilitate retrieving.

Market Gunner: One who hunted for the purpose of selling the game he killed, a practice now illegal in North America. A market hunter.

Mask: The head or pate of a fox, raccoon, wolf, or coyote.

Match Rifle: A rifle designed for competitive shooting, a target rifle.

Minute of Angle: This is the unit of adjustment on all telescopic, and most aperture, sights, being indicated by a series of fine lines. One minute of angle is equivalent to the following distances at the ranges indicated:

British and American		Metric	
25 yards	$\frac{1}{4}$in	25 m	.69 mm
50 yards	$\frac{1}{2}$in	50 m	1.39 mm
100 yards	1in	100 m	2.78 mm

Moor: High, treeless land such as that inhabited by grouse.

Mounts: Metal bases used to secure a telescopic sight to the barrel or receiver of a firearm.

Muzzle Brake: A device on the muzzle of a shotgun or rifle which, by means of vents and baffles, deflects gases to the rear to reduce recoil.

Muzzle Energy: The energy of a bullet or projectile on emerging from the muzzle of the firearm that discharges it. Usually designated in foot-pounds or kilogram-meters.

Muzzle Velocity: The speed of a bullet or projectile at the moment of emerging from the muzzle. Usually expressed in feet or meters per second.

O'Clock: A means of indicating a location on the target or over a range or field, corresponding to similar locations on the face of a clock, 12 o'clock being at the top of the target, or at the target end of the rifle range. Thus, a shot striking the target immediately to the left of the bull's-eye is a hit at 9 o'clock, and a wind blowing from the right at a right angle to the line of fire is a 3 o'clock wind.

Offhand: Shooting in a standing position, without the use of a rest or sling.

Over-and-under: Double-barreled firearm with one barrel superimposed over the other.

Palmated: Of the shape of the antlers of moose, caribou, and fallow deer that is similar to the shape of the palm of a hand with fingers outspread.

Pass-shooting: A form of shooting in which the hunter places himself in position under a known flyway or travel route of ducks, geese, pigeons, or doves. The birds are shot as they pass, without the enticement of decoys.

Pattern: The distribution of a charge of shot fired from a shotgun.

Pattern Control: Control of the shot pattern by means of choke.

Peep Sight: See **Sights.**

Peg: The numbered stick indicating the position of a shooter at a covert shoot or partridge drive.

Pelage: The fur, hair, or wool covering of a mammal.

Pellet: Round shot, of any size, a given number of which make up the shot charge.

Picker-up: One who, helped by dogs, finds and gathers what is shot.

Piece: The mid-day meal carried by a shooter.

Piston: In an automatic or semiautomatic arm, a metal plunger which, when forced down a cylinder by powder gases, operates a mechanism to extract and eject the fired cartridge, and to reload and cock the arm.

Pitch: This can be observed by resting a gun upright beside a wall with the butt or butt plate flat on the floor. If the barrel is exactly parallel with the wall, the gun is said to have no pitch. If the breech touches the wall and the barrel inclines away from it, the distance between the muzzle and the wall is the "negative pitch." If the barrel inclines toward the wall, so that there is a distance between the breech and the wall, this distance is what is called, simply, the "pitch." A pitch of 2 to 3 inches (5 to 8 cm) is desirable on a repeating rifle because it causes the butt to remain in place at the shoulder when the rifle is fired rapidly.

Point: The motionless pose assumed by a dog which indicates the proximity of game birds.

Points: The horn features of an antlered head which determine its ranking as a trophy (e.g. "a twelve-pointer" is brow, bay, tray, and three on top of each antler).

Point of Aim: The bottom edge of the bull's-eye for a target shooter using iron sights; the center of the bull's-eye for one using a telescopic sight.

Pointing Out: A method of shotgun shooting in which the shooter selects a point ahead of the moving target at which to shoot so that the shot charge and target will meet. Opposite shooting style to "swinging past."

Post Sight: See **Sights.**

Pot-hunter: One who hunts primarily for meat rather than sport.

Powder: The finely divided chemical mixture that supplies the power used in shotgun and metallic ammunition, technically propellant powder. When the powder is ignited by the flash of the priming composition it burns with a rapidly increasing gas which develops a pressure of 6,000 to 55,000 lb per square inch (420 to 3,900 kg per square cm) in the chamber and bore of the gun. This gas furnishes the propelling force of the bullet or charge of shot. Originally, all propellant powder was black powder formed in grains of varying size, with the size of the grain determining the rate of burning and suitability for various cartridges. Modern powders are smokeless and their base is nitroglycerine or nitrocellulose or a combination of both, the product then being called double-base powder. The rate of burning is controlled by the composition, by the size and shape of the grains, and whether or not coated with some retarding substance called a deterrent. Those so coated are called progressive-burning.

Primaries: The outer and longest flight feathers of a bird; quill feathers.

Primer: The small cup, or cap, seated in the center of the base of a centerfire cartridge and containing the igniting composition. When the primer is indented by the firing pin, the priming composition is crushed and detonates, thus igniting the charge of powder. Rimfire cartridges contain the priming composition within the folded rim of the case, where it is crushed in the same manner. The British term is cap.

Pull: The distance between the face of the trigger and the center of the butt of the gunstock. Also, the amount of pressure, in pounds, which must be applied to the trigger to cause the sear to disengage and permit the hammer to fall. Also, the command given to release a skeet or trap target.

Pump Gun: Common name for the slide-action rifle or shotgun. See **Slide Action.**

Quartering: A hunting-dog term for the act of ranging back and forth across the course.

Quartering Bird: A bird which approaches the shooter at an angle, either right or left.

Rat-tailed: Lacking long hairs on the tail, as in the case of such dogs as the Irish water spaniel.

Receiver: The frame of a rifle or shotgun including the breech, locking, and loading mechanism of the arm.

Receiver Sight: See **Sights.**

Recoil: The backward movement, or "kick," of the firearm caused by the discharge of the cartridge.

Recoil-operated: Of a firearm which utilizes the recoil, or rearward force exerted by the combustion of the powder, to operate the action and extract, eject, and reload to the extent of the number of rounds in the magazine.

Recoil Pad: A soft rubber pad on the butt of a firearm to soften its recoil.

Reduced Load: A cartridge loaded with a lighter than standard powder charge, for use at a short range.

Reticule (or Reticle): The crossed wires, picket, post, or other divisional system installed in a telescopic sight to permit its use as a gunsight, or in a pair of binoculars to permit the use of a scale for estimating distances.

Retrieving: Dog's act of finding and bringing an object, generally dead or wounded game bird, to the handler.

Revolver: Any handgun embodying a cylindrical magazine, as opposed to a single-shot or semiautomatic handgun, either of which is usually called a "pistol."

Rib: The raised bar or vane, usually slightly concave on its upper surface and usually matted, which forms the sighting plane extending from breech to muzzle of a gun. It is used on all double-barreled shotguns.

Rifle: A firearm projecting a single rotating bullet. Also, as the Rifle, the member of a stalking party who will fire the shot (cf. the Gun).

Rifled Slug: A bullet-shaped projectile with hollow base and rifled sides used in a shotgun for hunting big game. Will not harm shotgun barrels and will not "ream out" any type of choke.

Rifling: Parallel grooves cut into the bore of a rifle or pistol, spiraling from the breech to the muzzle, causing the bullet to spin in its flight.

Rig: A setting of decoys in front of a boat or blind; also used to describe the entire hunting outfit.

Rimfire: A cartridge in which the priming compound is contained in a rim at the base.

Ring Hunt: A form of driving in which a large number of shooters and beaters form a ring and gradually close in, to drive the game toward its center. An ancient method, still used in Europe, primarily for hunting hares and foxes.

Rough-shooting: The pursuit and taking of game and other quarry by Guns who have no human assistants but are generally aided by spaniels. See also **Dogging.**

Royal: Fourth point, after the tray and before the fifth, of antlers.

Royal Bull: A bull elk (wapiti) that has six points on each antler. A very desirable trophy. Also, royal stag of the European red deer.

Run: In some regions, a game trail or path created by animals over a period of time.

Safety: The device which locks a firearm against the possibility of discharge; sometimes called a safety catch. In common practice, the term applies primarily to the button, pin, or toggle which, when set in the "safe" position, prevents the discharge of the arm by pulling the trigger. A safety which automatically resets itself in the "safe" position when the gun is opened during the reloading process is called an automatic safety. Such a safety is most common on double-barreled shotguns.

Scapulars: The feathers on each side of the back of a bird's shoulders.

Scope: Telescope or telescopic sight.

Sear: The device in the lock of a firearm which holds the hammer or firing pin in its cocked position. When the trigger is pulled to the rear, it depresses the sear, which in turn releases the hammer or firing pin.

Secondaries: The wing feathers inside the primaries.

Semiautomatic: Any firearm which will fire, extract, eject, and reload by means of pressure on the trigger, but requires repeated pressure on the trigger to fire each round.

Set: A "rig" or setting of decoys.

Set Trigger: A trigger, the sear of which is "set up" by a preliminary movement or by pressure on another trigger, permitting the sear to disengage the hammer at the slightest touch or pressure on the trigger.

Most set triggers are adjustable for the amount of pressure desired.

Sewelling: Cords carrying colored streamers which, when activated, cause birds to flush far enough back to ensure that they are flying high when over the Guns.

Shell: Empty case of any cartridge. Also, an American term for a loaded shotgun cartridge.

Shock Collar: A collar with an electronic device which can be set off by remote control to give a dog an electric shock to punish it when it does not obey or does something wrong. The shock collar is a dangerous instrument in the hands of a novice trainer because it can ruin a dog when used incorrectly.

Side-by-side: A double-barreled shotgun with the barrels positioned side by side, as opposed to the over-and-under configuration.

Sight Radius: The distance between the front and rear sights. The longer the distance the greater the accuracy of the firearm.

Sights: The aiming device on a firearm. On most rifles and handguns, the factory-installed sights consist of two elements called "front sight" and "rear sight," which together frequently are called "iron sights" because they are made of principally metal. The front sight, located on the barrel near the muzzle, is usually post-shaped or bead-shaped and hence sometimes called post or bead. The rear sight is usually located partway down the barrel, near the breech or on the receiver. If it consists of a V- or U-shaped notch in a flat piece of metal, it is called an "open" sight. An open sight with a deep U-shaped notch with protruding wings is called a "buckhorn sight." The rear sight can also consist of an aperture in a disk. It is then called an aperture, or peep, sight. When the aperture sight is attached to the receiver it is called a "receiver sight" and when it is attached to the tang it is called a "tang sight." When the aperture adjustments have micrometer settings, such a sight is sometimes called a "micrometer sight." A hunting shotgun usually has only one sight consisting of a bead near the muzzle, but most trap and skeet guns have a second bead halfway down the barrel. There are also telescopic sights for rifles and handguns.

Sign: Any indication of the presence of game. Sign may include tracks, droppings, marks on trees, or any other indication that the area has recently been visited by a game animal.

Silvertip: Colloquial name for the grizzly bear.

Singing Ground: An open area used by the male woodcock for its courtship display.

Six o'Clock, or Six-o'Clock Hold: A term for the aiming point indicating that a rifle or handgun has been sighted-in to place the bullet not at the point of aim on a bull's-eye but well above it, so that the shooter aims at the center of the bottom edge. If the bull's-eye is a clock face, the point of aim is at 6 o'clock, but the impact point is at the exact center, midway between 6 and 12 o'clock. Target shooters prefer to aim in this way, when using iron sights, as it permits them to "rest" the bull's-eye on the top of the front sight and center the bull's-eye in the rear-sight aperture. See **O'Clock.**

Slide Action: A repeating firearm action in which the breech is closed and opened and the action operated by means of a sliding fore-end that acts as a handle for sliding the breech into the opened or closed position. Also **Pump Gun.**

Small-bore: Specifically, of a .22-caliber rifle chambered for a rimfire cartridge. Sometimes applied to rifles chambered for centerfire cartridges up to .25 caliber and shotguns under 20 gauge.

Smoked Sights: Sights after they have been blackened by soot from a candle or blackening lamp, thus eliminating any shine or glare. Commercial spray blackeners are also available.

Smoothbore: A firearm without rifling.

Sneakbox: A term for the Barnegat Bay duck-boat.

Spike-collar: A dog-training accessory—a slip collar with small spikes on the inside, used to force obedience to commands.

Spook (v): To frighten game. A term used by a hunter to indicate that a bird or animal flushed or jumped from cover at his approach, or when it winded or heard him.

Spooky: Of any animal or bird that is extremely wary or constantly alert.

Spoor: Tracks or footprints of animals. Sometimes used to mean all game sign.

Spotting Scope: A telescope with sufficient magnification to permit a shooter to see bullet holes in a target at long range, and to permit hunters to see game and evaluate trophy animals at long range. The average sporting scope is 24 power.

Spread: The overall area of a shotgun pattern. Also, the inside distance between right and left antlers or horns at their widest separation or at the tips.

Spy: An interlude of halting, waiting, and watching in which a deer shooter observes his quarry and its movements before deciding the tactics of his approach.

Stag: The mature male of the red deer.

Stalker: The professional who guides and advises those seeking to shoot deer on open forests in Scotland; also, a shooter of deer in woodland who approaches the deer by stealth.

Stalking: A method of hunting in which the hunter locates game and then stealthily follows a predetermined route to arrive within shooting range of the quarry.

Stanch: Firm and decisive; describing a dog's style while pointing. The dog that establishes a point and holds it, without caution or admonition, until his handler flushes his birds, may be regarded as stanch. Also spelled "staunch."

Stand: The position at which the shooters are placed for each drive at a covert shoot (hence "first stand," "second stand," etc.).

Start: The moment when a hound first finds scent or a trail.

Steady: Of a dog's behavior after birds are flushed. The dog is "steady to wing and shot" when he retains his position after the birds are flushed and the shot is fired.

Still-hunt: A method of hunting in which a hunter moves very slowly and silently through cover in search of game, pausing frequently to scan the terrain. The word "still," in this context, means silent rather than motionless.

Stock (n): The wooden part of a shotgun or rifle, or the handle of a pistol or revolver. The butt section of a stock is called a buttstock.

Stock (v): In game management or preserve operation, to stock is to release game in suitable habitat.

Stop: An assistant tactically placed to prevent pheasants approaching the shooters too closely, or evading them, at a covert shoot.

Swinging Past: A method of shotgun shooting in which the target is overtaken and passed by the sight, and the swing with the target is continued as the trigger is pressed. See **Pointing Out.**

Switch: A mature male deer whose antlers have no points.

Take-down: Of a firearm in which the barrel and adjacent parts can be readily separated from the receiver or action, thus permitting the arm to be packed in a short container.

Tang Sight: See **Sights.**

Team: An old British term for a flock or group of ducks.

Telescopic Sight: A telescope with reticule, permitting an aim of greater accuracy and clearness than that of an ordinary sight.

Tertials: The wing feathers inside the secondaries that are closest to the body.

Throwing Off: Of a rifle that is performing erratically or failing to give reasonable accuracy. This often results from improper bedding of the barrel.

Timberline: The upper limit of forest growth at high altitude.

Toe: The lower part of the butt of a shotgun or rifle.

Tolling Dog: A dog once widely used in Europe, and used now only in Nova Scotia, to entice wildfowl to enter a trap or to lure them within range of the gun. The action of the dog in running back and forth on the shore stimulates the birds' curiosity. In Nova Scotia, these dogs are bred to resemble a red fox and are registered by the Canadian Kennel Club as the Nova Scotia tolling retriever.

Trade (v): Of game, to move back and forth over a given area: "The ducks were trading along the far shore."

Trailer: A dog which continually or frequently follows his bracemate.

Trailing: Act of following game. See **Tracking.**

Trajectory: The course described by a projectile in flight. It forms an arc due to the effect of gravity. Usually, measured in terms of height above the line of sight at midrange.

Tray: The third point of antlers of a deer, after the brow and bay (or bez). The word is sometimes spelt "trez."

Trigger Guard: A guard surrounding the trigger or triggers of a firearm.

Trigger Pull: The pressure required to bring about the release of the sear notch on the hammer, permitting the hammer to fall.

Tularemia: A virulent disease, known also as "rabbit fever." Rabbits are its major victims, and great care should be exercised when skinning rabbits. The disease can be communicated to humans if a cut or scratch on the hands or arms makes contact with an infected animal. The disease can be fatal. No harmful effects result from eating of an infected bird or animal, as thorough cooking destroys the virus.

Turkey Shoot: Originally, turkey shoots utilized a turkey as a target as well as a prize. The bird was placed behind a shield with only its head protruding. In early turkey shoots, contestants were permitted one shot in the standing position at 10 rods (55 yards/50 m); later, the ranges varied. At modern turkey shoots, a regulation target is used or clay targets are thrown from a trap, the turkey going to the shooter with the best score.

Turning to Whistle: A hunting-dog term for breaking the cast and turning the dog in response to the handler's whistle.

Twist: The angle or inclination of the rifling grooves off the axis of the bore. Twist is designated by measuring the number of turns or fractions of turns to the inch of barrel length. A "14-inch twist" means that the grooves make one complete turn inside the bore every 14 inches (35.6 cm).

Upland Game: A general term for all small game, including birds and mammals.

Various: In Britain, fair but unexpected quarry for which no category is provided in normal game records (e.g. jay, gray squirrel).

Varmint: A colloquial American term (stemming from "vermin") for a generally undesirable animal. Woodchucks and foxes are widely considered varmints. In some regions, the term is also used for predators such as bobcats. However, many predatory and non-predatory animals that were formerly classed as varmints are now protected or managed as game animals.

Varmint Cartridge: Cartridge designed to give exceptionally good accuracy, high retained velocity, and consequently flatter trajectory. Varmint cartridges are so called because they were originally developed for long-range shooting at woodchucks and prairie dogs.

Varminter: A rifle employed primarily for long-range varmint shooting. Many such rifles have long, heavy barrels for maximum velocity and accuracy.

Velocity: The speed of a bullet or shot charge, usually designated in feet per second or meters per second.

Velvet: Soft vascular tissue which covers the antlers of deer until they have attained their full growth and form, at which time membranous tissue dies and is removed when the animal rubs its antlers against brush and trees.

Ventilated Rib: A raised sighting plane affixed to a shotgun barrel by posts, allowing the passage of air to disperse the heat from the barrel which would otherwise distort the shooter's view of the target. Very useful on trap and skeet guns.

Vernier Sight: A rear sight, the aperture of which is raised or lowered by means of a threaded post with a knurled knob. A vernier scale on the frame indicates the elevation in hundredths of an inch.

Walk-up: A shooting method, chiefly for partridges and grouse, in which the shooters and their companions advance in line through a crop, stubble or heather, taking birds as they flush.

Wild Flush: The rise of game birds for no apparent reason, usually far from the gun.

Wing: All feathered quarry. See **Fur**.

Winged: A term indicating that a game bird has been hit but not killed. Used primarily by upland shooters. See **Cripple.**

Yard: An area, usually within a forest, in which a large number of deer, moose, elk, or similar mammals herd together, tramping down the snow and feeding on the browse supplied by the low branches. Used especially by whitetail deer when snow becomes deep enough to impede normal travel through browse areas.

Yaw: To vary from a straight course. A bullet which does not travel exactly "nose on" but wobbles slightly sideways is said to "yaw."

Yeld: A female deer without offspring; if a red hind, and barren, generally the leader of the herd.

Zero: The adjustment of the sights on a rifle to cause the bullet to strike a calculated impact point at a given range. A rifle with the sights zeroed for 100 yards will, under normal conditions, place the bullet in the center of the target at that range.

Bibliography

ACKLEY, P. O. **Home Gun Care & Repair.** Harrisburg, Pennsylvania, 1969.

ANDERSON, L. A. **How to Hunt Small American Game.** New York, 1969.

BAILLIE-GROHMAN, WILLIAM A. and BAILLIE-GROHMAN, F., eds. **Edward of Norwich: Oldest English Book on Hunting.** Repr. of ed. of 1909.

BARBER, JOEL D. **Wild Fowl Decoys.** New York, 1934.

BARNES, F. C. **Cartridges of the World.** Northfield, Illinois, 1972.

BERNSEN, PAUL S. **The North American Waterfowler.** Seattle, Washington, 1972.

BEST, G. A. and BLANC, F. E., eds. **Rowland Ward's Records of Big Game (Africa).** 15th ed. London, 1973.

BOUGHAN, ROLLA B. **Shotgun Ballistics for Hunters.** New York, 1965.

BOVILL, E. W. **The England of Nimrod and Surtees: 1815–1854.** London, 1959.

BRISTER, BOB. **Shotgunning: The Art and the Science.** Tulsa, Oklahoma, 1976.

BURK, BRUCE. **Game Bird Carving.** New York, 1972.

BUTLER, ALFRED J. **Sport in Classic Times.** Los Altos, California, 1975.

CAMP, RAYMOND R. **The Hunter's Encyclopedia.** Harrisburg, Pennsylvania, 1966.

CAPSTICK, PETER H. **Death in the Long Grass.** New York, 1978.

CARMICHEL, JIM. **The Modern Rifle.** Tulsa, Oklahoma, 1975.

CHURCHILL, ROBERT. **Churchill's Shotgun Book.** New York, 1955.

CONNETT, EUGENE V., III. **Duck Decoys.** Brattleboro, Vermont, 1953.

COYKENDALL, RALF. **Duck Decoys and How to Rig Them.** New York, 1955.

DALRYMPLE, BYRON. **Complete Guide to Hunting Across North America.** New York, 1970.

—**How to Call Wildlife.** New York, 1975.

DANIELSSON, BROR., ed. **William Twiti's the Art of Hunting.** Atlantic Highland, New Jersey.

DARTON, F. HARVEY. **From Surtees to Sassoon: Some English Contrasts 1838–1928.** Darby, Pennsylvania.

DA SILVA, S. NEWTON. **A Grande Fauna Selvagen de Angola.** Luanda, Angola, 1970.

DE HAAS, F. and AMBER, J. T., eds. **Bolt Action Rifles.** Northfield, Illinois, 1971.

DELACOUR, JEAN. **The Waterfowl of the World.** 4 vols. London, 1954–64.

DORST, JEAN. **Field Guide to the Larger Mammals of Africa.** London, 1970.

DUFFEY, D. M. **Bird Hunting Know-How.** Princeton, New Jersey, 1968.

—**Hunting Dog Know-How.** New York, 1972.

EDMAN, IRWIN., ed. **Socrates' Passages in Plato's "Dialogues."** New York, 1956.

ELLIOTT, CHARLES. **Care of Game Meat & Trophies.** New York, 1975.

ELMAN, ROBERT. **1001 Hunting Tips.** Tulsa, Oklahoma, 1978.

—**The Hunter's Field Guide.** New York, 1974.

ELMAN, ROBERT., ed. **All About Deer Hunting in America.** Tulsa, Oklahoma, 1976.

ELMAN, ROBERT and PEPER, GEORGE., eds. **Hunting America's Game Animals & Birds.** New York, 1975.

ERRINGTON, PAUL. **Of Men and Marshes.** Iowa City, Iowa, 1957.

FALK, JOHN R. **The Practical Hunter's Dog Book.** New York, 1971.

FITZ, GRANCEL. **How to Measure & Score Big-Game Trophies.** New York, 1977.

FORRESTER, REX and ILLINGWORTH, NEIL. **Hunting in New Zealand.** Wellington, New Zealand, 1967.

GATES, ELGIN T. **Trophy Hunter in Asia.** New York, 1971.

GREENER, W. W. **The Gun and Its Development.** London, 1881. Repr. 9th ed. New York, 1968.

GRESHAM, GRITS. **The Complete Wildfowler.** South Hackensack, New Jersey, 1973.

HALTENORTH T. and TRENSE W. **Das Grosswild der Erde und Seine Trophäen.** Munich, 1956.

HEILNER, VAN CAMPEN. **A Book of Duck Shooting.** New York, 1947.

HENDERSON, L. M. **Pocket Guide to Animal Tracks.** Harrisburg, Pennsylvania, 1968.

[HERBERT, W. H.] **Frank Forester's Field Sports of the United States.** New York, 1849.

HERNE, BRIAN. **Uganda Safaris.** Tulsa, Oklahoma, 1980.

HINMAN, BOB. **The Duck Hunter's Handbook.** Tulsa, Oklahoma, 1974.

HULL, DENISON B. **Hounds and Hunting in Ancient Greece.** Chicago, Illinois, 1964.

JOHNSGARD, PAUL A. **Waterfowl, Their Biology and Natural History.** Lincoln, Nebraska, 1968.

KNAP, JEROME. **Where to Fish & Hunt in North America: A Complete Sportsman's Guide.** Toronto, Canada, 1970.

KOLLER, L. **Shots at Whitetails.** New York, 1970.

KRIDER, JOHN. **Krider's Sporting Anecdotes.** Philadelphia, 1853.

MACKEY, WILLIAM J., Jr. **American Bird Decoys.** New York, 1965.

MARTIN, ALEXANDER C.; ZIM, HERBERT S.; and NELSON, ARNOLD L. **American Wildlife & Plants.** New York, 1951. MARTIN, ALEXANDER C., ed. Repr. ed. New York, 1961.

MELLON, JAMES et al. **African Hunter.** New York, 1975.

O'CONNOR, JACK. **The Art of Hunting Big Game in North America.** New York, 1977.

—**The Hunting Rifle.** Tulsa, Oklahoma, 1970.

—**Sheep and Sheep Hunting.** Tulsa, Oklahoma, 1974.

ORMOND, CLYDE. **Complete Book of Hunting.** New York, 1972.

ORTEGA Y GASSET, JOSÉ. **Meditations on Hunting.** New York, 1972.

OWEN, T. R. H. **Hunting Big Game with Gun and Camera.** London, 1960.

PETERSON, ROGER; MOUNTFORT, GUY; and HOLLOM, P. A. D. **A Field Guide to the Birds of Britain and Europe.** 3rd ed. London, 1974.

PETERSON, ROGER TORY. **A Field Guide to the Birds.** Boston, 1947.

—**A Field Guide to Western Birds.** Boston, 1969.

PETZAL, DAVID E., ed. **The Experts' Book of the Shooting Sports.** New York, 1972.

—**The Experts' Book of Upland Bird & Waterfowl Hunting.** New York, 1975.

REID, WILLIAM. **Arms Through the Ages.** New York, 1976.

REIGER, GEORGE. **Wings of Dawn.** New York, 1980.

RICE, F. P. and DAHL, J. I. **Game Bird Hunting.** New York, 1965.

ROURE, GEORGES. **Animaux Sauvages de Côte d'Ivoire.** Abidjan, Ivory Coast, 1962.

RUE, LEONARD L., III. **Sportsman's Guide to Game Animals.** New York, 1969.

SCOTT, PETER. **A Coloured Key to the Wildfowl of the World.** Slimbridge, England, 1957.

SPRUNT, A., IV and ZIM, H. S. **Pistols, A Modern Encyclopedia.** Harrisburg, Pennsylvania, 1961.

STEPHENS, WILSON. **The Guinness Guide to Field Sports.** London, 1978.

STEWART, J. and STEWART, D. R. M. "The Distribution of Some Large Mammals in Kenya." **Journal of the East African Natural History Society and Coryndon Museum** 24 (June 1963). Nairobi, Kenya.

SURTEES, R. S. **The Analysis of the Hunting Field.** New York, 1966.

TERRES, JOHN K. **Flashing Wings: The Drama of Bird Flight.** New York, 1968.

THOMAS, GOUGH. [GARWOOD, G. T.] **Gough Thomas's Gun Book.** New York

—**Gough Thomas's Second Gun Book.** New York 1972.

—**Shooting Facts & Fancies.** London, 1978.

TRENCH, CHARLES CHENEVIX. **The Desert's Dusty Face.** Edinburgh and London, 1964.

VILLENAVE, G. M. **La Chasse.** Paris, France.

WATERMAN, CHARLES F. **Hunting in America.** New York, 1973.

WELS, B. G. **Fell's Guide to Guns and How to Use Them.** New York, 1969.

WHITEHEAD, G. KENNETH. **Deer of the World.** New York, 1972.

WOLTERS, RICHARD A. **Water Dog.** New York, 1964.

WOOLNER, F. **Grouse and Grouse Hunting.** New York, 1970.

YOUNG, GORDON. **Tracks of an Intruder.** New York, 1970.

Index